The Trust Imperative

The Trust Imperative

Practical Approaches to Effective School Leadership

Andrew Dolloff

THE SCHOOL SUPERINTENDENTS ASSOCIATION

ROWMAN & LITTLEFIELD
Lanham • Boulder • New York • London

Published by Rowman & Littlefield
An imprint of The Rowman & Littlefield Publishing Group, Inc.
4501 Forbes Boulevard, Suite 200, Lanham, Maryland 20706
www.rowman.com

86-90 Paul Street, London EC2A 4NE, United Kingdom

British Library Cataloguing in Publication Information Available

Library of Congress Cataloging-in-Publication Data Available

ISBN 9781475862188 (cloth : alk. paper) | ISBN 9781475862195 (pbk. : alk. paper) | ISBN 9781475862201 (epub)

∞™ The paper used in this publication meets the minimum requirements of American National Standard for Information Sciences—Permanence of Paper for Printed Library Materials, ANSI/NISO Z39.48-1992.

In honor of my father, whose thirty-six years as a teacher and high school principal in one community serve as an enduring model of ethical, trust-filled leadership, and my mother, whose unwavering efforts as a public servant in that same community continue as she approaches eighty-five years of age.

With gratitude to Brenda, my greatest supporter, primary editor, and an outstanding teacher in her own right. Those who read this book just once will gain great appreciation for her persistence, resilience, and loyalty in reading it multiple times.

For Mariah, Caleb, Megan, and Kristen—whose accomplishments and risk-taking activities as young adults are already staggering. I can't wait to see where your lives lead next.

Contents

Preface

Having had the opportunity to serve as a school leader for the past twenty-five years, mostly as a high school principal and superintendent of schools, I must admit that for many of those years I had never really identified why we did things the way we did. The schools in which I worked performed well (by most measures) and feedback from staff, parents, students, and the community were overwhelmingly positive. Like most school leaders, my days were consumed with a vast array of activities that left little time for thoughtful reflection about each interaction I had with constituents. Why I adopted certain approaches to various opportunities and challenges was not something I spent enough time analyzing.

It wasn't until I started teaching leadership at the graduate level that I was challenged to clearly define my own core beliefs about leadership. Through preparing for each class, exploring leadership theories, and reading my students' papers, I began to better define why certain approaches to school leadership were more effective than others, as well as identify areas within my own performance that varied from those core beliefs and called for a shift in practice.

As those beliefs came into focus more sharply, and as I had the opportunity to observe, mentor, and learn from other school leaders, it became clear that the single most important value of successful leadership is trust: not just trust *of* the leader *by* constituents, but trust *between and among* all members of the school community. Where trust is strong, schools thrive. Where trust is broken, schools struggle to meet their mission. The need to foster a pervasive sense of trust among the greater community is a simple concept, but a difficult task requiring intentional, empathetic, willful, and intelligent effort.

By understanding there is opportunity to either build or disassemble trust in every moment of the day, leaders take a significant step toward improving student learning. From there, deliberate effort can be made to lay a foundation of trust throughout the school that encourages collaboration, innovation, and high levels of staff and student engagement.

Throughout this book, I share ideas and observations made through three decades of school leadership. Some of the best ideas are those I saw others employ, while some of the faux pas are mine alone. In either event, details have been omitted to protect those who would rather not be identified.

I don't share any of this as a proclamation of my own proficiency as a leader, as I continue to learn each day of better ways to do things. Rather, I share ideas as a way to spur the reader's thinking about their own interactions, so they might discover and develop their own effective practices for fostering trust and improving student experiences in their schools.

My hope is that the reader will find in these pages a suggestion or two that will help them better serve students. My intention is to further the conversations we have about school leadership—with others and inside our own minds—so that we may provide the direction, facilitation, and inspiration our communities need to meet our students where they are and get them started on the path to what's next.

Chapter 1

The Importance of a Trust-Filled School

In the people-oriented business of schooling, trust is the make-or-break characteristic that determines the effectiveness—and longevity—of the leader.

Exceptional leadership of complex organizations comprised of large numbers of diverse constituents is challenging work regardless of the setting. When that organization is a school, where hundreds of families send their children to be nurtured and inspired each day—and where dozens of skilled professionals engage passionately in caring for those children—the challenge is particularly acute.

Schools require both a foundation and a framework of trust if they are to provide innovative, equitable opportunities in a setting where students feel safe and valued. Educational leaders play a critical role in ensuring that trust permeates every layer of the school, beginning by demonstrating the trust they have in others, then fostering the trust others have in them as leaders, and finally, growing the trust all constituents have in the school as an organization.

Schooling is a people-oriented business; the relationships formed *inside* the organization have a significant and lasting impact on constituents *outside* the organization. The school thrives when its people thrive—when they feel physically and emotionally safe, when they are comfortable sharing ideas and taking risks, when they are empowered to be innovative and collaborative, and when they are encouraged to engage in learning through failure.

Human resources are the school's most valuable capital. This includes most notably students, teachers, and administrators. It also includes parents, bus drivers, nutrition workers, paraprofessionals, office staff, custodians, and many other individuals who work at, or interface with, the school on a daily basis. The school leader is tasked with working with each of these groups to ensure high-quality opportunities are provided for, and accessed by, each student each day.

The perspectives and experiences of a vast range of constituents are wide and varied, and relating to each requires a tremendous amount of interpersonal acumen. School leaders must recognize that forging and capitalizing on those relationships is the only way to promote and sustain a culture of trust, which provides the strong foundation needed for continual school improvement.

RELATIONSHIPS: AT THE CORE OF SCHOOL IMPROVEMENT

Educators have long believed, and various researchers have confirmed, that the quality of instruction in the classroom is the single most impactful resource schools contribute to student achievement. Indeed, a school may have the most updated curriculum, the latest textbooks and instructional materials, and the newest technology, but if the teacher in the classroom isn't a clear communicator or doesn't relate well with the students, learning will be minimized. Conversely, if the teacher in the classroom is an expert instructor, it matters very little which textbook is used or whether each student has a laptop to take home; the students will have a meaningful experience.

To measurably impact student learning, the school leader must influence instruction—and that is done most effectively when trusting relationships allow for safe discussions centered around teaching and learning. The greatest challenge for the school leader is not to pick the right textbook for each classroom, but to facilitate a collaborative effort in which each student is nurtured and empowered to reach their greatest potential. It is the relationships formed between staff and students that most significantly impact student learning, just as it is the relationships formed between the school leader and staff that most impact the school's collective effort to attain its mission.

Developing trusting relationships with staff in the building is clearly not the only challenge for the school leader. That same level of care must be demonstrated to nurture trust among students, families, and the community at large. When students feel unsafe, unseen or unvalued at school, learning is impaired. When parents lack confidence in the school's intentions and efficacy, progress is slowed. When the community questions the school's efficiency and oversight, resources become constrained.

This is the challenge that lies at the feet of the school leader, and the stakes are high. Schools must be bastions of equity and creators of opportunity, for without effective schools, only the privileged advance, the less fortunate are left behind, and achievement gaps widen. School leaders are entrusted with much—from the academic, emotional, and physical well-being of students to the efficient use of community resources—and they must heed the call to foster trust in every aspect of the role in order to bring about sustainable growth for the school and its students.

TRUST: THE FOUNDATIONAL ELEMENT OF EFFECTIVE LEADERSHIP

Embarking on this journey to ensure that staff and students are provided the support and encouragement they need each day may seem daunting at first. Interactions with hundreds of school leaders over the past twenty-five years have shown they are clear in their understanding that the work requires vision, collaboration, and communication. They know it requires a culture of professionalism and continual improvement. Most notably, leaders at schools where collaboration and empowerment produce uncommon results consistently identify a pervasive sense of trust as the most important component of the school's culture.

For many Americans, Watergate marked a point in the nation's history when the public's trust in its leaders, already in decline after eight years of controversial American involvement in Vietnam, took a sharp dive.[1] Although there have been a few upticks at specific moments in history when patriotism has surged (e.g., shortly after the 9/11 tragedy in 2001), the enduring trend for Americans has been diminishing trust in leadership—and in one another—for the past half-century.

By 2018, 75 percent of Americans sensed a fading trust in the federal government and 64 percent sensed a fading trust in one another.[2] Although local school leaders have historically been among the most trusted of all public officials, this widespread and growing lack of trust is surely being felt in superintendents' and principals' offices throughout the nation.

Paul Zak, professor of economics, psychology, and management at Claremont Graduate University, has been studying the relationship between organizational trust and performance for more than twenty years. Through one study, Zak and his colleagues found that respondents who worked at companies where trust was perceived to be high reported less stress, more energy, higher productivity, fewer sick days, greater life satisfaction, and less burnout than those in lower-trust environments. Employees in higher-trust companies enjoyed their jobs more, felt more aligned with the company mission, and were more engaged with their colleagues.[3]

The implication of Zak's work for schools is clear: students and teachers in high trust environments will be more likely to show up, focus, collaborate, and give their best effort than those in schools where trust is less palpable. Zak is not a voice in the wilderness on this front. Liz Ryan, a Forbes contributor and former Fortune 500 senior vice president for HR goes so far as to say, "Every problem companies experience with their employees springs from the same root cause: there is too little trust in the environment."[4]

To better understand the need for a trust-filled organization, one might imagine what schools look like when trust has been damaged. Unfortunately, a plethora of examples can be found simply by perusing the headlines of local and national media outlets on almost any given day:

- *Students protest district's message to teachers*
- *Parents storm board meeting to protest diversity plan*
- *Fed-up teachers, parents make their voices heard at school board meeting*
- *Teachers cast no-confidence vote for superintendent*

Of course, there are many factors that could have led to each of these headlines, so it may be unfair to say there is an absence of trust in each case. However, one can imagine each of these stories playing out quite differently if trust were in abundance. In schools where leaders recognize the importance of trust and where relationships are at the core of all decisions, it is less likely that disagreements will escalate into protests, lawsuits, and changes in personnel—and more likely that they will be discussed, mediated, and settled without fanfare, reducing the noise that distracts the school from its mission.

In *The Speed of Trust*, Stephen M.R. Covey (2006) calls trust "the one thing that changes everything" and "the key leadership competency of the new global economy."[5] Like Zak, Covey's writing is focused on business leaders, but is clearly applicable to the people-oriented business of schooling, and is supported by educational researchers such as Douglas Reeves, who identifies trust as one of seven essential elements of successful school leadership.[6]

Highly effective leaders understand the need for trust throughout all circles of the school community, realizing that in every interaction trust may be either fostered or weakened. Where there is doubt, cynicism, and fear, educators retreat to their silos—be that a classroom or an office—advising colleagues to "keep your head down and stay off the radar." Where there is trust, teachers and administrators assume the best intentions and capabilities of one another and feel empowered to collaborate, share ideas, and try new approaches in emotionally safe spaces.

As illustrated in figure 1.1, school leaders have tremendous influence regarding the level of trust with which their organization is viewed, as they are at the relational center of the school. They are among the few whose daily work brings them into contact with members of each constituent group in the school—staff, students, families, and community members. School leaders

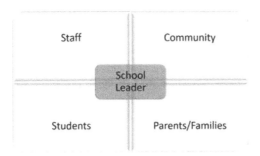

Figure 1.1   The School Leader at the Relational Center of the Organization. *Source:* Author created.

who view themselves at the center—as a conduit between various constituent groups—rather than at the top of a hierarchical order, will be better suited to build the trust necessary to turn their school into a highly functioning organization.

This is an important concept to understand at the outset of this exploration of trust-building practices in the school setting. Leaders who only view themselves at the top of the school's power structure will struggle to implement the strategies suggested throughout this text. While there are certainly times when hierarchies are properly employed and the school leader must be the decision-maker, there are many more settings throughout the school day and year when the leader must interact authentically as a member of the team, supporting, guiding, facilitating, and learning alongside others as the situation warrants.

It is important to recognize that while the leader is at the relational center, this does not mean their needs should be at the center of the school's focus. Clearly any school leader who places their needs ahead of the students has much more to learn than this simple text may provide. The skilled leader operates from the center while keeping the needs of others at the top of the priority list.

To maximize effectiveness from the center, the leader must be comfortable working alongside and among all constituents. Students, staff, parents, and community members each have a unique relationship with the school leader, providing powerful opportunities and demands for the leader to foster trust in authentic and meaningful ways. From casual interactions with students in the school lobby to public presentations in front of hundreds of families or citizens, school leaders are called upon to nurture trust in the organization in all settings. Leaders must take deliberate action to ensure that trust grows, rather than wilts, in each instance.

Throughout this book, readers will be encouraged to consider approaches to school leadership that build trust in every moment with each constituent.

Recognizing the need for a trust-filled organization is the first step toward creating one. The journey continues by exploring core interpersonal competencies of trust-building leaders. Significant portions of the text will then focus on specific strategies that build trust with various constituent groups (staff, students, families, and the community). Finally, a chapter on trusting one's self and creating a healthy lifestyle will serve as a motivating point from which to put these ideas into practice.

NOTES

1. *Public Trust in Government, 1958-2019.* 2019a. Pew Research Center. Washington, DC. https://www.people-press.org/2019/04/11/public-trust-in-government-1958-2019/.

2. *Trust and Distrust in America.* 2019b. Pew Research Center. Washington, DC. https://www.people-press.org/2019/07/22/trust-and-distrust-in-america/.

3. Reprinted by permission of Harvard Business Review. Excerpt from "The Neuroscience of Trust" by Zak, Paul. January–February, Copyright © 2017 by Harvard Business Publishing; all rights reserved. https://hbr.org/2017/01/the-neuro-science-of-trust.

4. Ryan, Liz. 2018. "Ten Ways to Build Trust on Your Team." *Forbes*, March 17, 2018. https://www.forbes.com/sites/lizryan/2018/03/17/ten-ways-to-build-trust-on-your-team/?sh=2faa762c2445

5. Covey, Stephen M.R. 2006. *The Speed of Trust.* New York: Free Press.

6. Reeves, Douglas. 2016. *From Leading to Succeeding.* Bloomington, IN: Solution Tree.

Part I

BUILDING TRUST THROUGH PERSONAL COMPETENCIES

Chapter 2

Empathy, Integrity, and Ethical Leadership

Muddled leadership demonstrates empathy but lacks integrity. Authoritative leadership demonstrates integrity but lacks empathy. Ethical leadership demonstrates both empathy and integrity—and that's what our schools need.

Leaders in all sectors of the economy are called to provide ethical leadership by communicating a clear purpose for their organization and modeling individual accountability to high personal and professional standards. The call for ethical leadership is particularly loud in America's schools. While public leadership at the national level is often rancorous and oppositional, leaders at the local level are challenged to rise above the examples perpetuated on social media, television, and radio and exhibit the ethical leadership that constituents trust.

Ethical leadership is steady and just. It seeks out, recognizes, and values the needs of individuals while furthering the mission of the organization. It is trustworthy, equitable, and uplifting, requiring a unique blend of a wide range of characteristics. Honesty, humility, courage, compassion, curiosity—these are but a few of the required traits of the ethical leader. Above all else, the ethical leader must demonstrate integrity and empathy—not to offset one another, as the two are not mutually exclusive—but with large quantities of each.

It is not uncommon for school leaders to be characterized as persons of *integrity*. Indeed, they live in a world of rules, regulations, accountability measures, and public scrutiny, and their longevity in the profession may often hinge on their ability—and willingness—to adhere to the standards and policies that are spelled out for them regardless of who is watching. In the world of social media, the call for integrity in the school leader is more pronounced than ever before, and more than one administrator has suffered a fall from grace after demonstrating a lapse in judgment that may have gone viral.

At the same time, there is a growing demand for *empathy* in leadership, especially within schools, as greater focus is placed on social-emotional support for students and staff, as well as equity, diversity, and inclusion for all constituents. Leaders are tasked with responding to the unique needs of hundreds of individuals in order to provide each with their best opportunities for improvement and learning.

School leaders must be prepared to evaluate and understand the inequities that exist in their instructional and programmatic frameworks—something that can only be done through an empathic evaluation of the organization. How leaders respond to this demand will contribute greatly to the level of trust by which they are viewed by all constituents.

LEADING WITH INTEGRITY

Leaders with integrity act with consistency in each situation, allowing others to predict how they will respond and taking the guessing game out of interactions between the leader and their constituents. However, being consistent is not enough; integrity-driven leaders are also principled and introspective—admitting to mistakes, holding themselves accountable to the truth, and making choices in the best interest of others. Such leaders are trustworthy—their staff know they will be true to their word, their actions will back their words, and they would make the same decisions behind closed doors as they would in front of a public audience.

Clearly, one who leads with integrity is on the correct path toward successful leadership; however, there is more they must consider in order to lead the organization to its greatest potential—they must also lead with empathy, and it is in that effort that many leaders fall short.

LEADING WITH EMPATHY

To empathize is to envision oneself in another's shoes, to understand that their perspective may be different from one's own, and to have some desire to help them, if possible, because of an inward sense of compassion. The empathetic leader creates trusting relationships that elicit loyalty from their colleagues; staff want to perform at their best not out of a sense of accountability, but because they don't want to let down a leader they admire and respect.

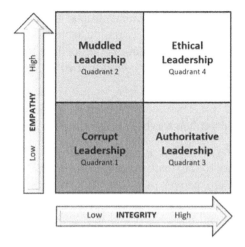

Figure 2.1   Four Quadrants of Ethical Leadership. *Source*: Author created.

Figure 2.1 illustrates the shared importance of empathy and integrity. As shown here, in order for leaders to provide ethical leadership, they must exhibit high degrees of both integrity and empathy. One without the other is better than having neither, but a leader who lacks one or the other cannot provide the ethical leadership necessary to help the organization reach its greatest potential.

Integrity and empathy need not be in competition with one another, though it may often seem as though acting with one requires dismissing the other. A school leader who upholds the integrity of every rule and policy may miss the opportunity to demonstrate empathy in an unusual situation, while one who favors bending the rules frequently will eventually weaken the integrity of the organization. Applying the appropriate measure of integrity and empathy in every situation is necessary to create a culture of trust, while displaying only one of these two important characteristics leads to less effective leadership as described below.

Quadrant 1: Corrupt Leadership (neither Integrity nor Empathy)

Hopefully, in the people-oriented business of schools, leaders with neither integrity nor empathy are moving rapidly toward extinction. Narcissistic individuals in this quadrant have one person's best interests at heart: their own. They are often intelligent and talk a good game, but more often than not, the initiatives they start are mere resume-builders as they use each job as a stepping stone to the next. When they display empathy, it is because it benefits them, and when they show integrity, it is because it benefits their agenda.

Employees soon learn to be cautious around these individuals. They are often skilled enough to convince a significant number of constituents that they are operating in Quadrant 4, but over time, their true colors will appear. With little to no sign of empathy or integrity, it will be clear that their motives and actions are corrupt.

Quadrant 2: Muddled Leadership (High Empathy, Low Integrity)

Imagine leaders who are wonderfully empathetic but struggle to maintain the integrity of the school. They care deeply for their staff and attempt to understand each individual's perspective when they are presented with requests or guidance. The staff feel supported and valued as individuals; they authentically like the leader and want to do their best as a result.

However, because the leader tends to support every idea and is intent in each moment to make every individual happy, there is a sense that decision-making is muddled; the organization is rudderless, appearing to head in whichever direction the wind blows, with no strong hand at the helm maintaining a consistent course.

About these leaders, it is often said, "They make their decision based on whoever they talked to last." Staff soon learn how to manipulate decisions—as do parents and students—as the leader's empathy extends to all constituents. The leader is stuck in leadership Quadrant 2: Muddled Leadership. The integrity of the organization is broken, and the school flounders as decisions are no longer consistent, predictable, or mission-focused.

Quadrant 3: Authoritative Leadership
(High Integrity, Low Empathy)

It is not uncommon to hear frequently about leaders on the other side of this coin—persons of high integrity who are consistent, honest, and mission-focused. These leaders operate consistently in Quadrant 3: Authoritative Leadership, giving the policies and protocols of the organization high priority in all decision-making exercises.

Leaders in this quadrant have a firm grasp on the reins and are unwavering in their application of policy. They often speak about "maintaining high standards" and fear "setting a precedent" when asked to consider exceptional situations. They write policies to address as many scenarios as possible so that the integrity of the organization is maintained and individual requests can be made to easily fall within the parameters of the rules, thereby greatly reducing the need for them to make a judgment call.

However, schools are filled with human beings who come to the building with a wide variety of needs and experiences that are not easily ignored for the duration of the instructional day. To act only with integrity, foregoing empathy, results in an authoritative leadership style that can take the school only part of the way toward its mission.

Quadrant 4: Ethical Leadership (High Integrity, High Empathy)

To provide ethical leadership at the highest level, leaders must act with both integrity and empathy, understanding what is most needed in each situation. Approaching a staff member who consistently arrives at school later than is required calls for integrity (holding all employees to professional standards) as well as empathy (showing concern and a willingness to make accommodations for an individual who may be facing difficulties at home). The most effective leaders understand the call for a balanced approach and strive to maintain the integrity of the organization while demonstrating empathy for the individual.

DEVELOPING DEEPER EMPATHY AND INTEGRITY

Some may believe that these qualities are innate; a person is either born with integrity or not, or they have empathy or not. While it is true that all people are born with certain qualities that exist somewhere on a continuum, the growth mindset of educators and leaders should provide hope that individuals can develop greater empathy and integrity even as mature adults. Leaders should practice a range of activities to move further into Quadrant 4 and the realm of ethical leadership.

1. To develop greater integrity:
   * Create a personal credo. Identify things worth standing for and stick to that credo in all settings. Write the statement down and keep it where it can be viewed on a regular basis. Reflect on it each day, and especially in trying moments, as a way to remain centered on those values that are of importance, both professionally and personally.
   * Read more books about leaders who demonstrated great integrity in the face of difficult challenges. Nelson Mandela, Abraham Lincoln, Ruth Bader Ginsburg, and Condoleezza Rice are a few whose stories inspire in many facets of leadership. Studying the lives and decisions of individuals at the highest levels of leadership can be inspirational and informative for leaders in any field.

- Foster relationships with people of integrity and avoid those whose honesty or motives are questionable. The company one keeps has a great impact on one's own actions, beliefs, and behaviors. Leaders should surround themselves with people who are admired for all the right reasons and challenge themselves to meet the standards their colleagues demonstrate.

2. To demonstrate greater empathy:
   - Develop more inquisitive questioning skills. Asking others for more information when they come forward with ideas or dilemmas can help a leader develop greater empathy for their position and perspective. Leaders who find this particularly challenging may want to start out by developing three or four questions before heading into a planned meeting. With time and practice, the questions will come organically as positive experience is gained.
   - Explore unintended biases. This may require more effort than almost any other tip in this book and will likely require the help of others. Leaders must start by understanding what it is that defines them as well as how they define others. Equity and inclusion will be discussed later in chapter 9, but an introspective consideration of personal biases should begin now.
   - Put some energy each day into knowing the staff better. Leaders should learn about individual employees' families, their history, or their interests outside of work. A starting point is to set a goal of learning one thing about one staff member each day. Soon, the leader will be engaging with constituents throughout the organization on a different level.

Before turning to chapter 3, take some time to consider the need for ethical leadership in schools and how individual behaviors leave leaders stuck somewhere in Quadrants 1–3. Specifically, leaders should reflect on their responses to the following questions:

1. When a staff member or student makes a request for special consideration regarding a deadline, expectation, or policy, how much consideration should be given to past practice or precedent-setting concerns versus the need for flexibility and compassion?
2. What is more important, the Golden Rule ("treat others the way you would like to be treated") or the rules of the school? In other words, does upholding the integrity of the school's policies outweigh the need to treat each case individually?

3. After making a decision that requires balancing empathy with integrity, which would cause greater consternation: showing greater empathy or holding tight to integrity?

There are no absolute answers to many of the challenges school leaders face. However, taking time to consider the call for empathy and integrity while making dozens of decisions and interacting with hundreds of constituents each day should help school leaders better locate their own ethical compass and chart a course for trust-building leadership.

Chapter 3

Restraint, Composure, and a Call for Civility

You don't have to swing at every pitch.

Many school leaders have experienced the excitement, frustration, and satisfaction of overseeing a school construction project. From the earliest stages of concept planning to acceptance of the occupancy permit, building a school is an educational adventure like none other. One of the most exciting days in this process occurs when the contractor begins pouring the building's foundation. This is a critical step in the process, as the concrete must be set under the proper conditions of temperature and humidity and allowed time to cure before any structures are erected overhead.

Several safeguards are in place to ensure the foundation can support the building's weight. If any measurements show the structure to be inadequate, decisions must be made as to the proper solution, which may include anything from letting it stand as is, reinforcing it, or ripping it out and starting all over.

Imagine if these measurements and tests are taken only after the building is fully constructed on top of the flawed base. Replacement of the foundation would require either tearing down of the structures placed on it or installing elaborate supports to hold the structures in place while repairs are made. Clearly, it is far better to take the time to lay the foundation properly than to rush the job, believing it can be patched up later, if necessary.

The same principles apply to the decision-making structures and relationships within the school; neglecting to construct a foundation of trust for the organization will make every task much more difficult, requiring significant reinforcement and support of others until the foundation is rebuilt. While strategies for building trust with different constituent groups will be discussed in later chapters, this chapter will provide insight into two critical characteristics school leaders must display outwardly at all times in order to lay a foundation that can withstand stress tests, hazardous conditions, and heavy loads: *restraint* and *composure.*

INTERPERSONAL RESTRAINT

A foundation of trust requires civility in all settings. Leaders who model civility create in others a stronger desire to collaborate and adopt the mission of the school than those who struggle to provide constituents with the respect and attention they deserve. Too frequently, news outlets carry stories of tumultuous situations resulting from actions taken by school leaders that, upon reflection, simply should have been avoided. In most cases, if the leader had just not made one particular statement, not sent a certain email, or refrained from responding in anger and frustration to a specific situation, the ensuing maelstrom would never have developed.

Restraint, then, must be considered one of the critical characteristics of a trust-building leader. Self-regulation in the treatment of others and in the decision-making processes of the school must be demonstrated at all times, lest the leader be viewed as impetuous, impulsive, and impatient.

Those who tend to react quickly and verbally in many situations may appreciate the advice a seasoned superintendent once gave to his inexperienced high school principal. Having been appointed to the position in his early thirties, the principal had not had much life experience regulating his responses to others. He showed little patience for conversations that were, in his own estimation, a waste of time.

His impatience was particularly visible at weekly district-wide administrative meetings, where principals from each of the district's schools sat with central office leaders to set and manage the course for the district. As the district had only one high school and multiple elementary schools, the high school principal often felt isolated in the perspective he shared from the secondary level, and he struggled to mask that frustration with diplomacy.

After one meeting in which he had voiced his displeasure with something that had been said by one of his colleagues, the principal stepped into the superintendent's office to reiterate his concern. The superintendent, a former high school principal himself, interrupted after a few seconds and said, "You know, you don't have to swing at every pitch."

"Come again?" the principal asked.

"Let a few go by," the superintendent said. "Sometimes people just need to know that they've been heard, and if they say something that you disagree with, that's okay. What they say may not have any bearing on the final decision we make as a district—it's just their opinion, and you'll have your chance to share yours. Just try to be a bit more diplomatic in how you work with them; you might even find them agreeing with you from time to time."

This approach is necessary in all areas of school leadership. Whether interacting with students, parents, staff members, or the public, restraint is a critical characteristic of effective school leaders. With so many highly charged situations in schools each day, and a tremendous amount of work to be accomplished, it is easy to respond quickly to ideas, suggestions, and questions. Offering rapid responses and consistently providing answers—as opposed to being contemplative and asking questions—are two sure signs that a leader needs some practice using restraint.

ORGANIZATIONAL RESTRAINT

Building trust through restraint is not just about interpersonal communications—it is also about organizational direction. The leader who lacks restraint when considering potential new programs will take on too many initiatives, draining energy from the staff and adding confusion where clarity is needed most. Constituents will sense the lack of direction and lose trust that the mission is being adhered to. The leader will quickly be accused of resume-building, dismissing tradition, and jumping at every "shiny new thing."

Consider the experience of one leader who decided within months of assuming a new position that the school should abandon its decades-old grading processes in favor of a standards-based reporting system. While the leader was certainly not alone in recognizing the benefits of a more personalized and descriptive assessment and reporting structure, many in the school community did not have a firm understanding of how the proposed change would benefit students, and they feared it would negatively impact their students' chances of gaining acceptance at their colleges of choice.

Lack of understanding and fear of change led many in the community to a place of wary suspicion of the leader's competence (at best) and motives (at worst). Opposition swelled from students, parents, and staff. A public conflict ensued in which the school community lost sight of the central theme of the debate, leading to character attacks and accusations of mismanagement of the district. Within months, the initiative was dead—and will likely remain so until the leader has built the trusting relationships necessary to allow such a change to grow organically from within the ranks of the school professionals.

This unfortunate outcome was avoidable had the new leader understood the call for organizational restraint and foundational trust. Rather than giving in to the temptation to bring about *immediate* change, leaders should focus on the goal of making *lasting* change. Rushing in to make change without having laid a foundation of trust to support that change, leaders forfeit years of impact. A far more effective approach is to focus on relationships first, encouraging thoughtful reflection on best practices, and nurturing innovative ideas from members of the school community who will help pave the way for meaningful change among all constituents.

COMPOSURE

"Controlled chaos" is how many describe the school day, and it is a fitting label. Schools are complex organizations comprised of hundreds of individuals arriving at school via dozens of modes of transportation, entering facilities that have a multitude of complex systems—all of which provide opportunities for disruption. Threats against the school, errant fire alarms, student conflict, and the potential for critical situations are constant concerns for the school leader. Even in the highest-performing schools, administrators regularly take a deep breath at the end of each day, relieved that they have reached that point once again without injury or disaster.

While the maturity required to restrain from reacting too quickly in everyday situations is important, there will be times when responding to critical situations requires immediate action, yet action that is tempered with restraint. How leaders respond in times of crisis may define them in the eyes of others for a significant portion of their careers. Every such situation is an opportunity for leadership; in fact, it is a demand for leadership. Composed, measured responses give others confidence that the leader has the situation under control, providing the type of leadership they are comfortable following.

PUTTING IT INTO PRACTICE

Demonstrating restraint and maintaining composure in high-stress situations is a challenge for many leaders. By their very nature, most educational leaders are fixers; they want to help people, they want to solve problems, they seek truth and fairness in all matters, and they feel a great deal of personal responsibility for the safety and welfare of all students and staff. None of these attributes is necessarily bad, but they can get in the way of empowering others to grow, to participate authentically in the search for solutions, or to reach the truth on their own—all actions that build trust.

To strengthen performance, leaders must boost their own capacity for restraint and composure by considering several strategies that reduce the likelihood of impulsivity:

1. Practice mindfulness.

School leaders often find themselves in emotionally-charged situations, and many of those situations occur in the public eye, either formally or informally. A reserved temperament will build trust, while a quick tongue earns the leader a reputation as a hothead, a reactionary, or worse.

When facing a potentially heated exchange, leaders must count to ten, take a breath, or employ any number of mindful strategies that promote a measured response. "Speak now, or forever hold your peace" only applies at weddings; school leaders must recognize that they will have opportunities to impact matters of importance on a regular basis, and immediate responses to complex or emotional situations are not always necessary.

Holding one's tongue is typically a better approach than acting in the heat of the moment. While responding *thoughtfully* to questions, ideas, proposals, or accusations is important, responding *immediately* is not. In fact, instantaneous responses may be emotional, rushed, and lack the reflection, accuracy, and diplomacy necessary to foster trust with the recipient.

2. Don't overshare.

Often, through nervousness, insecurity, or any number of reasons, school leaders share more information than necessary which, in many instances, leads to more questions and more opportunities to misspeak or misinform. Finding that balance between keeping others informed and sharing too much is an acquired skill for many leaders.

One strategy for developing this talent is to observe the recording of one's own presentations or participation in a meeting and reflect on the following questions:

- Could pertinent information have been shared more succinctly?
- Was all *important* information, but only *relevant* information, shared?
- Did the information shared provide clarity or raise more questions?

Leaders who provide concise, factual information without a great deal of hyperbole or extraneous language build trust by providing others with the data they need without dominating the conversation.

3. Ask questions.

Rather than rushing to a response in each situation, more effective leaders continue seeking information. This demonstrates thoughtfulness and an interest in what others have to share. Creating a list of questions from which to launch conversations will help each leader develop questioning skills that invite others to share information. Two basic questions to consider asking at all times are:

- Is it good for kids?
- How does this align with our mission and core values?

4. Give it time.

In today's world of rapid communication, leaders are bombarded with requests, complaints, notifications, and updates. Email, voicemail, interoffice mail, and traditional mail provide constituents with virtually endless access to school leaders. Previous generations managed this much better than today's leaders, likely because communication moved at a slower pace. The mail came once a day, creating a contained time frame during which to review the new arrivals. Then came phone messages, requiring someone to write out the messages and report them to the intended party. Voicemail and email came next, and the expected timeline between receiving and responding became tighter.

Today, instant notifications on cell phones and mobile devices create a false sense of urgency about almost every message received. Responding within minutes can create the unrealistic expectation that school leaders will be available 24/7 when the fact is, many messages can sit a day or so before receiving a reply, providing the leader the opportunity to craft a thoughtful response.

5. Recognize that not every communication requires a response.

Often, leaders will be included in communications that do not require their immediate attention and may be resolved by others without their input. Giving others an opportunity to manage concerns at their level is empowering and demonstrates faith in their judgment. If it goes sideways, the leader will typically have an opportunity to help get things back on course.

6. Understand that not every problem can be fixed by the leader alone.

Oftentimes, the solutions to a problem are better understood by someone else, if given the opportunity to respond. When the leader responds first, those with more knowledge, experience, or insight into the particular challenge may withhold their thoughts, respecting the authority of the leader too much to offer a different solution, no matter how healthy their relationship is.

7. Think of the school as a customer service organization.

It is important to remember that many who interact with a leader may not know them intimately enough to understand the leader's sense of humor or other aspects of their personality. Some will automatically assume negative things about school leaders simply because they are "the boss." Leaders must do everything in their power to not perpetuate those negative stereotypes and to project an image for the school and community that is consummately professional. Leaders in a particularly contentious situation may want to consider having someone not emotionally engaged in the matter review correspondence before it is sent.

8. Consider everything but adopt few things.

As an organization, taking on every great idea results in confusing priorities, strained resources, and staff fatigue. Sticking to a few, focused initiatives that are tied strongly to the school's mission and supported by data allows for greater concentration of effort and a unified approach to the work. This approach promotes avoidance of top-down mandates by seeking widespread input before new programs are adopted.

9. Anticipate and drill.

Since the devastating events at Columbine High School in 1999, schools have placed great emphasis on mitigation, preparation, and response plans for emergency situations. Having a solid plan in place with frequent, well-planned drills allows the school's occupants to respond in a calm, measured manner during a live event. While leaders should not let fear and hysteria dominate the culture within the school, a systematic approach to planning and drilling allows for a more organized response when the alarm sounds.

Anxiety and frustration will build quickly if tasks such as finding emergency contacts or accessing rapid communications systems take too long during an emergency. Constructing an organized response plan, with all necessary resources readily accessible will allow the leader to focus on the major decisions that need to be made, rather than searching for email addresses and phone numbers in the heat of the moment.

Acting with restraint, both in interpersonal communications and in the adoption of new ideas and programming, is a challenge for many leaders—especially those who are new to the role. The temptation to act quickly and decisively may be alluring in the short term, but often leads to disempowerment of others and an authoritarian culture that is beneficial in only the rarest of settings.

Leaders who fail in this challenge will place their school on shaky ground, with a lack of trust at its core. Laying a proper foundation takes time and planning. It is possible to go back and strengthen that foundation by adopting strategies such as those suggested here but rebuilding the base once the structures are in place is perilous, and leaders are well-advised to lay a strong foundation before implementing significant change.

Stressful situations—from intense faculty meetings to threats of physical harm to the school—can be either trust-building or trust-crumbling events. Remaining the calmest person in the room while efficiently addressing the myriad details that arise in such events is one sure way to develop confidence with constituents, while responding hysterically breaks down any trust that has been previously developed. Preparing for those stressful situations will allow the leader to respond in a composed manner that strengthens the foundation of trust critical to the organization.

Chapter 4

Courage

Knowing what needs to be done is often the easiest part of leadership; having the courage to see it through is the greater challenge.

Possibly more than at any point in our nation's history, it seems every decision—either in the private or public domain—elicits a political response. From allowing school-day student protests of school shootings to requiring face coverings during a global pandemic, school leaders navigate rugged terrain each day, and the moves they make will almost always be met with criticism from one faction or another. How leaders prepare for and respond to criticism will go a long way toward determining their effectiveness.

Yielding to criticism in a manner that leads one to abandon difficult work may compromise the school's core beliefs and lead to a breakdown in trust of the school leader. Responding to criticism with both an open mind and firm resolve is necessary. To bow to critics and abandon decisions at every turn results in a lack of focus; to ignore them results in inflexibility. Neither is a desired characteristic for those intent on building trust, and it takes courage to respond with the proper combination of willingness to reconsider a position and the professional conviction to stand firm when necessary.

IMPROVING INSTRUCTION

While educator effectiveness policies have proliferated in recent years, it was not long ago that teachers and school leaders could work in the profession for decades with limited—or nonexistent—formal evaluation protocols. A teacher might have been observed two or three times in their first few years in the classroom and then allowed to teach for decades without being provided any feedback on their performance.

In one such school, the newly hired principal discovered not only that veteran teachers were not being observed, but also new teachers who had been hired in recent years were given only cursory, largely positive reviews and—at the end of their probationary periods—issued continuing contracts without much impetus for improving their methods. Recognizing the opportunities that were being missed for shaping and improving the school's instruction, the principal began implementing the evaluation and supervision model defined in the district's policies.

This required the school leadership to have a much greater presence in classrooms than had been experienced previously, along with a noticeable increase in teacher participation in pre- and post-observation conferences. The principal also worked with other administrators to develop meaningful ways to communicate areas of needed improvement, balancing critical feedback with supportive statements and offering opportunities for professional development.

The response from teachers in the early stages was concerning. Teachers felt they were being watched and that a lack of trust was being displayed by the new administration. The principal responded that she was merely implementing the district policy and there was no better way to ensure quality instruction throughout the school than to see teachers in action every day and increase dialogue about their classroom practices. The principal reassured the staff that observations were not about catching people doing things wrong, but rather a key component of focusing on continual improvement. Warily, teacher leaders agreed to support this new focus.

Unfortunately, the implementation of consistent observations exposed weaknesses in one new staff member that were unable to be overcome and, with several months remaining in the school year, the principal had to make the difficult decision not to extend her teaching contract for the following year. The teachers' association immediately sent representatives to meet with the principal, where they declared that this was highly unusual—no teacher had been withheld a continuing contract for as long as these veteran teachers could remember. Surely this would rock the confidence of the teaching staff and negatively impact morale throughout the school.

The principal was under a good deal of stress in this moment. The veteran teachers expressing their concern were excellent instructors and positive contributors to the school through their work in and out of the classroom. They had supported the principal during the hiring process and in every other setting during her initial year in the position. It would be quite comfortable to take the path of least resistance and reassess the decision not to renew the teacher's contract. Teacher morale wouldn't be threatened, and—according to these veterans—their confidence in the principal would increase.

The principal reflected for a few moments before responding but eventually was able to articulate that this decision, and each decision made going forward, was going to be about what is best for kids. And, based on the need for many supportive conversations held with the teacher in question throughout the year, the principal felt it was in her best interests as well, as the stress and strain of teaching was simply not something that she appeared equipped to handle.

As for the rest of the staff, the principal presented the position that a move such as this should not damage staff morale. In fact, it should boost morale when teachers realized they had a principal who valued their expertise and recognized that not just anybody can walk in off the street and do what they do every day. And with that, the principal held firm to the original decision.

The teachers left the meeting with a different understanding of the principal's perspective. Their empathy for the young teacher had not waned, but the logic of the principal's argument was not easily dismissed. In the end, the young teacher found employment in a field outside of the classroom, a new instructor was hired who was better equipped to meet student needs, and over time other teachers were reinforced by the support they received through the evaluation process.

This situation worked out for the principal, the teachers and the students because the leader demonstrated integrity over the long haul, following through on the promise to implement the evaluation model as one of support while hiring and developing excellent instructors and making decisions that benefit students, first. However, without the luxury of hindsight over the longer term, the most important quality for the principal to demonstrate throughout the early stages of this dilemma was courage.

In his research on highly effective leaders, Jim Collins identifies courage—in the form of professional willpower—as one of two required characteristics of the most competent leaders.[1] There is no doubt of the applicability of this concept to school leaders. With their decisions debated, dissected, and analyzed publicly, school leaders face a unique level of accountability. The lingering effects of these criticisms depend largely on the leader's courage to remain steadfast in doing what is best for kids.

DEMONSTRATING COURAGE AT WORK

School leaders are challenged to demonstrate courage in a variety of situations. Doing so is made easier when they employ a few general strategies that promote consistency and communication.

1. Hold everyone to the same clearly communicated standards.

One of the most challenging aspects of the job for school leaders is the implementation of behavioral and performance standards for students and staff. One of the first questions asked by those whose performance is addressed will be, "Where does it say I can't do that?" While policies cannot possibly describe every specific behavior expected in the school, articulating clearly the standards expected is an important first step in providing the school leader with the support needed to uphold those standards.

2. Pick up the phone or meet face-to-face.

Some educators have become reliant on technology for the purpose of communicating difficult information to parents. Automatically generated discipline notices are sent by email or messaging programs, allowing the administrator to meter out discipline with minimal interaction with parents. School leaders claim this is more efficient or that students need to be introduced to the concept of personal accountability without parental interference, but the result of overusing electronic communication is a reduction in the opportunities for positive interactions by creating a system in which only the most intense complainants are spoken to.

By calling parents more consistently, educators begin developing relationships, finding common ground, and collaborating on solutions. For students who end up in the office on a consistent basis, a bond formed between the school and home may be seen as a significant motivator for improved behavior. Those bonds are not formed through letters and emails, but through listening to one another and conversing respectfully.

The same is true for staff communications; emails and blanket memos allow the leader to avoid difficult personal interactions. These messages are easily misinterpreted or even dismissed by those who most need to heed their message.

Take, for example, the veteran teacher who struggles to arrive at school in a timely fashion. Nearly every day, the teacher rushes into the building as students are headed to their classrooms, even though the expectation that teachers be in their rooms well ahead of students is clearly stated and agreed to by all.

The approach some may take is to send out a building-wide memo reminding staff of the need to arrive at school by the appointed time each day. Others may choose to do this through an announcement at a staff meeting. Both of these approaches leave the staff bewildered, as the vast majority of them are meeting the standard each day, and they are not sure for whom the message is intended. Worse yet, the offenders are allowed to continue the behavior, comforted by the fact that they will not be personally challenged to make an adjustment.

This leads to a breakdown in trust among other staff members, as they would like everyone held to the same standard by which they are abiding, and they lose respect in the leader's ability to do the job. The message received is either (1) all employees can do as they please with no fear of reprisal or (2) certain employees can do as they please with no fear of reprisal. Either way, trust in the leader—and in the organization—is diminished.

The courageous leader goes about changing personal behavior in the most effective manner—through personal interactions. A conversation with this teacher may reveal something about their personal challenges that leads to a collaborative approach to problem-solving. Are they struggling with a difficult situation at home? Do they have an ill family member who requires assistance each morning? Issuing blanket statements or assuming that the teacher is simply derelict in their duties dismisses the challenges they may be facing. Using discretion, the leader fosters trust with the individual and avoids fostering mistrust with the larger staff.

3. Model what is expected of others.

The courage to expect more from others grows when one is able to ask only from others what they are willing to do themselves. Expecting anything less from oneself than is expected of others begins to break down the leader-follower trust. The school leader is particularly subject to this rule, due to the democratic nature of schools.

In one high school, teachers requested parking spots, as they felt too many students and visitors were arriving early and taking spaces closest to the school. The principal was opposed to the idea, believing it highlighted a hierarchy that she did not want to promote. The only problem was the parking spot closest to the main entrance had a sign posted in front of it that stated, "Reserved for Principal."

When asked about this dichotomy, the principal stated that she had to leave the building for district-level meetings and other functions on a regular basis, and she needed to be able to return to the school and park near the office; a reasonable response, but not one that engendered collegiality among the staff.

School leaders are challenged to be servant leaders. Little things like giving up a parking spot close to the door may not create a cultural shift within the school, but not doing so is one more unnecessary straw on the camel's back.

4. Be willing to show vulnerability.

The most courageous leaders are those who face up to their own weaknesses and are willing to grow and learn alongside others. The importance of owning up to one's mistakes and publicly accepting blame for the mistakes of others in the organization will be discussed more fully in chapter 5.

5. Collaborate.

Courage is demonstrated in the ability to work alongside others, rather than assuming positional authority based on titles and hierarchical structures. Leaders who let ideas develop from others, rather than forcing their own agenda, will build greater trust through empowerment of constituents.

6. Hire the best.

Possibly the most telling sign of leaders who lack courage is when they hire only individuals they believe to be good followers to those positions closest to them. This is demonstrated consistently in weak leaders who fear hiring someone who will outshine them among the faculty, students, or community. To avoid this, they hire others to whom they feel superior, or those they believe will be easily bent to their will, ensuring their own ego remains intact. Courageous leaders recognize that hiring individuals with greater and more diverse strengths will only bolster the organization's performance.

On a personal level, being surrounded by "Grade A" performers encourages growth in the leader (to be discussed further in chapter 10). Combining the desire to learn from others with the willingness to recruit and hire the best people available, leaders demonstrate the courage to address their own weaknesses and delegate responsibility where necessary.

Leadership takes courage. President Harry Truman once described it as "making those 51%–49% decisions" that few are thrilled with. School leaders who make intentional efforts to demonstrate courage will interact more authentically with constituents at all layers of the organization, building trust each step of the way.

NOTE

1. Collins, J. C. 2001. *Good to Great: Why Some Companies Make the Leap . . . and Others Don't.* New York: HarperBusiness.

Chapter 5

Intentional Trust

The greatest indicator of a leader's commitment to stand behind *their employees is their willingness to stand* in front *of them when fingers are being pointed.*

Once school leaders understand the critical nature of fostering trust throughout all levels of the organization, they often contemplate how to begin generating the trust they hope for others to have in them. This isn't a bad place from which to begin a journey of reflection, but the first step has less to do with actions leaders take to get others to trust them and more with the things they do to demonstrate trust in others.

This approach mirrors the fifth point in Dr. Stephen R. Covey's classic self-improvement text *The Seven Habits of Highly Effective People*, where he advises readers to "seek first to understand, then to be understood."[1] Covey's point transfers well to leadership theory, as leaders must understand that the first step in gaining trust *from* others is to demonstrate trust *in* others. When constituents feel trusted, they will be more likely to give trust in return, and they will be motivated to affirm the trust their leader has shown in them, maintaining a path of continual improvement for the entire organization.

For many school leaders, showing trust in others prior to seeing evidence that such trust is warranted is a difficult challenge. Taking on a new leadership position, many struggle to relinquish control of decisions that come their way each day. This is understandable; the pressures of the job, the vast opportunities for missteps across all levels of the organization, and the potentially public nature of any controversies that arise can be a recipe for disaster. Leaders may have many viable reasons to micromanage a situation, but the attempt to control every decision will diminish trust throughout the school and derail progress toward the mission.

ASSUMING COMPETENCE

School leaders must start the job, and each new year, assuming good intentions and a high degree of competency among the staff. When asked about their employees' motivations and capabilities, school leaders who understand the importance of trust at the core of the organization believe that the vast majority of educators care deeply about what they do and strive to put forward their best effort for students each day. Leaders who recognize this from the first moment on the job interact differently with staff than mistrustful micromanagers.

Trusting leaders allow staff members to do their jobs, providing themselves the time to focus on their own tasks. Leaders who are unable to trust are unable to give up control, detracting from their ability to accomplish their own duties, hindering others from feeling empowered to complete theirs, and sowing seeds of mistrust throughout the school.

Taken to its extreme, micromanagement is simply an untenable leadership strategy in an organization as large and complex as a school. The leader who employs this approach will soon be overwhelmed with all that needs to be done each day, losing sight of the school's mission and how to accomplish it. It has been said of these individuals that they are like the captain rearranging the chairs on the deck of the *Titanic*. While chaos ensues around them—and disaster looms just ahead—they are mired in the "administrivia" that serve little purpose in advancing the mission of the school. The chairs look nice— they just never reach their destination.

When advised to start from a position of trust in others, some leaders might ask, "What about those who aren't doing their best for students each day? If we just trust everyone implicitly, won't we be overlooking those who perform poorly?" Fear not—these individuals will appear on the radar soon enough. And when they do, the leader will have the opportunity to address each situation with dignity, which can serve to further deepen the trust staff has in leadership. In fact, such situations often lead to a growth in trust—not only with the individual whose performance must improve but with others who have been carrying the load for them.

When staff recognize that they are trusted and that they and their colleagues will be held accountable in a dignified manner, trust will spread through the organization in a sustainable way. Rather than acting as a compliance officer for each member of the staff, school leaders can expend such energy only with those individuals who are in need of more direct management.

Addressing Those Who Need Addressing

When dealing with those who have made an error or used bad judgment, trust-building leaders do so directly and respectfully with the individual, avoiding the proclamation of blanket statements that leave staff members confused or offended. This is exemplified by the school leader who was working in the office one summer day and noticed that a member of the faculty had brought a dog into the school while preparing his classroom for the coming school year. The principal found this to be problematic due to the fact that some staff members may have allergies or a fear of dogs.

Unfortunately, rather than speaking to the teacher in that moment, the principal sent a memo to every teacher in the building, reminding them that pets are not allowed in the building. The note consisted of a single paragraph, with several words underlined to emphasize the principal's displeasure.

Upon receiving the note, faculty were curious as to who had brought the dog into the school and why the entire staff had received the admonishment. The individual who had brought the dog to school wondered why he had not been addressed privately. The principal lost the respect of the staff, as they expected their leader to be able to address minor, isolated incidents in a more professional manner. The leader had taken unfortunate blanket action that diminished the trust others had in her.

To assess competency in this area, leaders should contemplate the following:

- Do I start each year, and each day, assuming the best intentions and capabilities of our staff?
- How can I better demonstrate trust in the staff, so they feel the confidence I have in them?

After identifying tangible responses to the second question, the reflective leader should think about asking these questions of others in the organization as a first step toward strengthening that foundation of trust. Honest responses may provide the leader with a different perspective and allow for a reallocation of personal resources (time, energy, and expertise) that leads to greater efficiency.

Sharing the Load and Allowing for Mistakes

It is not uncommon to hear school leaders bemoan their seventy-hour work week, and while it cannot be argued that school leadership is a nine to five job, an honest accounting would indicate it does not need to be an all-consuming one either. Leaders who micromanage and struggle with delegation find themselves spending far too many hours at work. This is an unsustainable approach to leadership, which leads to resentment of one's job, lack of a personal life, and a dysfunctional organization.

One sure way to make the job more manageable is to trust colleagues to do their work, encouraging experimentation and cultivating innovation on the front lines rather than in the front office. Leaders who feel overwhelmed by the time it takes to do the job each week should consider the level of trust they have placed in others by asking themselves two questions:

- Where might I be too controlling?
- What am I doing that I could trust to be done by others, without my direct input or oversight?

Once a list is generated, the leader can reassign tasks better done by others, empowering individuals to take ownership of items in their area of expertise. Consistent check-ins allow the leader to demonstrate interest in the work, while leaving the completion of tasks to others—unless they ask for or clearly demonstrate the need for assistance or guidance.

Make It Someone Else's Idea

If this message has not been delivered strongly enough in recent years, this is another plug for collaborative leadership, inviting the school community to engage in decision-making processes—from crafting the school's mission to implementing instructional programming to defining professional standards and student expectations. Mandates and directives are a sign of mistrust *by* the leader, fostering distrust *of* the leader.

One recent case involves an inexperienced leader who attempted to implement a district-wide change in school start times. The plan was developed largely at the leadership level, with little input from constituents throughout the district. While the proposal had been well-researched and had a great deal of merit, it would have resulted in an impactful shift in the routines of nearly every employee, student, and parent in the district. When the plan was unveiled to the public, those shifts raised the temperature in the community as vocal opponents to the plan became critical of the leader at school board meetings and in the local press.

Had the leader pressed the pause button at this point and sought greater community input, the plan may have been salvaged, albeit with some modification. Unfortunately, the plan was one for which the leader sought credit, rather than collaboration, and was therefore not explored with sufficient community and staff voice. The public outcry eventually crushed the initiative before it got off the ground as distrust spread throughout the district.

With thoughtful communication, a willingness to collaborate, and lack of need for personal recognition, a sound idea backed by solid research should not have been so easily dismissed. When a directive for sweeping change comes from the central office without input from the teachers or larger community, it is likely to be met with resistance. When that resistance is put down by an administrative power play (use of authority, local policy, or state statute), trust is decimated. Successful leaders present the data that suggest a better way of doing business and allow the ideas for that new direction to come from others.

Leaders seeking to gauge their own willingness to recognize the collective wisdom in their organization should consider these two questions:

- When I have an idea for improving our schools, how do I give others a voice in critiquing or improving that idea?
- Am I willing to let my ideas be adjusted and credited to another individual or the larger group?

Further self-reflection occurs when leaders pay attention to their own willingness to let an idea develop organically from others, rather than driving the conversation themselves. Leaders must recognize the collective wisdom of the team. When leaders provide members of the organization with the data and resources to fully study a problem, it is likely they will arrive at the best solution through a rich discussion that results in greater buy-in, a well-rounded plan, and a greater sense of trust among members of the team.

Building Trust through Error Management

Douglas Reeves states that one of the key components of building personal trust with staff is to "acknowledge one's mistakes quickly and openly."[2] Leaders who fail to recognize this need will suffer declining trust each time a denial is issued. The difficulty of admitting to one's mistakes as a school leader is compounded by the public nature of the job. Ironically, fear of looking weak can cause hesitation or avoidance altogether, which is weakness at its most basic level. Strength is demonstrated by the leader who stands in front of constituents and the public and says, "This was my decision, and it was the wrong one."

One of the lasting lessons from the Watergate scandal that resulted in the resignation of President Richard Nixon was that attempting to cover up a crime will bring down the leadership in the organization faster than the crime itself. Americans dislike dishonesty in their public officials more than they dislike incompetence. The public is frequently willing to accept mistakes so long as those mistakes are owned by those who made them—and so long as improvements are made. The smallest error compounded by denial or blaming can rapidly lead to public shaming, loss of trust, and a change in leadership.

The trust pyramid illustrated in figure 5.1 identifies how leaders build trust among constituents when errors are addressed within the organization. Depending on who made the error, the leader has the opportunity to foster individual and organizational trust by effectively learning from and taking ownership for the mistake.

Level 1: Helping Others Learn from Their Mistakes

Helping colleagues and students make improvements in their performance in a dignified manner is the first layer of fostering trust through error management. Effective leaders do this behind closed doors with those needing redirection. These moments provide unique opportunities for developing deeper trust with constituents who may or may not be the best performers. If they are habitual offenders, it may be that deeper trust is what is needed to help them change course and buy into the school's mission more fully. Many school leaders are effective at this level, as one of the basic tasks of any educator is to encourage learning through experience.

While educators often understand the need to develop trusting relationships with those students who can be most disruptive to the school, that philosophy is frequently left behind as they assume leadership roles in which they must supervise adults. This may be because leaders feel adults can be treated with less patience than children, but the effect is the same; building trust with these

Figure 5.1   Building Trust through Error Management. *Source*: Author created.

individuals will make them better performers, strengthening the organization by bolstering the weakest performers.

Level 2: Learning from One's Own Mistakes

While staff and students may be forgiving of leadership errors, leaders who make the same mistakes over and over again will quickly lose the trust and confidence of their constituents. Admissions and apologies begin to ring hollow if the leader does nothing to avoid similar mistakes moving forward. The old adage "'tis better to seek forgiveness than permission" is only applicable for one or two instances before staff members sense a pattern, which leads to a decline in trust. Just as schools are expected to be places of learning for students, so too must they be places of learning for school leaders.

To learn from one's mistakes, one must first be able to recognize those errors, and even low-performing leaders may learn from their mistakes in isolation; a more significant step toward maximizing trust-building is admitting to those mistakes publicly—or at least to those that have need to know, which leads to the third level of error management.

Level 3: Publicly Accepting Responsibility for One's Own Mistakes

The pyramid illustration might be more accurate with a double line between levels two and three, as it seems this is the point at which many leaders are left behind. An inability to admit to one's own errors will put an immediate halt on any expansion of trust in an organization, and it is here where many leaders are hampered by their own insecurities.

Leaders at the third level openly acknowledge their missteps and make authentic efforts to improve performance. This is an outward display of confidence that will engender greater trust from the staff and community. The most effective leaders set themselves apart by reflecting on times when they could have done better, exhibiting vulnerability and self-confidence— two preferred qualities of those in positions of authority. Leaders must think about the trust and confidence they have in themselves by contemplating these questions:

- When was the last time I stood in front of the staff and said, "My mistake"?
- What were the last three mistakes I made, and what did I learn from them?

An honest and humble assessment of one's own performance allows a leader to develop self-trust, which leads to greater trust from others.

Level 4: Publicly Accepting Responsibility for Others' Mistakes

At the highest level of building trust through error management, leaders accept responsibility not only for their own mistakes but also for mistakes made by others in the organization. This is a sign of a strong, ethical leader—one in whom others will place their confidence—and is one way a leader demonstrates both integrity and empathy with a single action. With thousands of interactions and hundreds of decisions being made by educators each day, there are countless opportunities for someone in the organization to make a misstep. Taking the heat for those missteps is part of the job for the effective leader.

Publicly accepting responsibility is so rare today; school leaders will find the approach to be quite disarming to those who come to levy complaints against the school. By taking the blame, the administrator immediately begins rebuilding trust with constituents, while deflecting criticism away from employees will foster loyalty and spur them to better performance.

To contemplate their willingness to take responsibility for the organization and all of its employees, school leaders should consider two questions:

- Can I identify instances where I have let an employee take the fall for something they did—and was that the best approach for my leadership and for the school?
- Can I identify a time when I clearly stood in front of the faculty or the public and accepted the blame for someone else's mistake, without giving any indication of who that person was?

Leaders with the confidence and courage to stand in *front* of their employees, as well as *behind* them, will nurture trust and loyalty that does not exist in organizations that play the blame game, where leaders point fingers at others and shrug off any responsibility they may have for making a bad call. Without trust, the school is stagnant—or worse. By trusting the staff, sharing the load, distributing credit, and owning personal and organizational mistakes, leaders begin to develop the individual and organizational trust necessary to bring about continual improvement for the school.

NOTES

1. Covey, Stephen R. 1989. *The Seven Habits of Highly Effective People.* New York: Free Press.

2. Reeves, Douglas. 2016. *From Leading to Succeeding.* Bloomington, IN: Solution Tree.

Part II

FOSTERING TRUST WITH SCHOOL STAFF

Chapter 6

Staff Relations

Remember from whence you've come.

If there is one constant that rings true in schools, regardless of their location, it is that there is not enough time in the day to do all that needs to be done. Teachers and school leaders jump on the professional treadmill each morning, turn it up to full speed and sprint through the day dashing from class to class and meeting to meeting, filling every moment with (hopefully) meaningful activity that furthers the school's mission.

When talking to educators at the elementary or secondary level about the challenges of their job, it is this lack of time that is the most consistently identified frustration. School leaders are in a unique position to address this challenge, but it requires awareness and intentionality to do so.

Leaders must recognize that *time to do the work* is the most valuable commodity that can be provided for staff, and its importance is too often disregarded. There is little opportunity to provide educators with meaningful compensation in other ways. Neither the annual operating budget nor the collective bargaining agreement likely allows for monetary reward, and those strategies typically lead to less unity among the staff, rather than more.

While much of the time in the teachers' day is defined, there are numerous opportunities throughout each week for school leaders to provide relief for many who are burning the candle at both ends. Administrators who waste those opportunities, or, worse, strive to fill every moment in a teacher's day, may permanently destroy any chance for a trusting relationship with the staff.

Two very different approaches to staff meetings highlight this concern. At School A, the leader fills each staff meeting agenda with items that may be easily announced through a memo or announcement sheet, ensuring that each meeting lasts for as long as the teachers' contract allows. Teachers sense that the meeting is being facilitated to ensure that they do not have time to work on their own. At the end of these meetings, staff aren't motivated to do their best for the leader—they are motivated to go home, frustrated by the lack of professional courtesy demonstrated by their leader.

At the other end of this continuum is School B, where the leader recognizes that instructors are spending significant time outside of the school day developing lesson plans, reviewing curriculum, and assessing student work. For this administrator, any time given back to teachers is an investment in her people. Rather than forcing the staff to attend unnecessarily long meetings, this administrator ends meetings early, allowing the staff to use the rest of the day as they see fit. Even more noticeable are the days when the meeting is set aside altogether, providing staff with an hour or two that they didn't plan on having.

Leadership staff in another district report that they have a standing weekly meeting with the superintendent lasting three-and-one-half hours. Staff throughout the district wonder what their building leaders could possibly be doing for that long. These leaders are absent from their buildings for more than 10 percent of weekly instructional time. It is a dangerous example to set, possibly leading to a district full of leaders who measure their value by the time spent sitting in meetings. In such a system—where nothing gets done without a meeting—the demand on employee time is strained, and face-to-face interactions with the wider staff and students are minimized.

The impact of giving staff the gift of time is immeasurable. A teacher who was planning on correcting papers all evening is instead able to finish work at school and dedicate some time to family, personal wellness, or other interests. Others are able to spend time collaborating on an instructional unit that would usually require giving up one's individual prep time or spending another late afternoon at school. On the intangible side, staff will come to trust that the leader will only ask for their time when it is necessary to do so, making them more willing to offer their energy to a project when asked.

There are many lessons to be learned about leadership, and hundreds of strategies to try in order to improve staff morale, but none may provide more palpable results than giving staff time they didn't think they had. To maximize those opportunities, leaders should consider the following strategies:

1. Avoid meeting for the sake of meeting.

The fact that recurring meetings are scheduled throughout the year doesn't mean each session needs to be held. If the agenda is full of informational items that can be shared electronically, leaders should send them out as announcements and cancel the meeting for that date.

2. When the meeting is over, let it be over.

The school is a collection of professionals. Although collective bargaining agreements exist for a reason, leaders must recognize that the vast majority of educators are working well beyond the number of hours indicated in their contract. Demonstrating this understanding in a tangible way by avoiding wasting time in meetings will go a long way toward building credibility and trust with the staff.

3. Have the courage to defend the staff.

The argument that someone may see a teacher at the post office or the grocery store in the early afternoon after the instructional day, is a hollow one. In the unlikely event that such a complaint is registered, the school leader must have the conviction to state how dedicated the staff is, and how far beyond the contract day they are working. If communities want to begin counting educator hours, they should be prepared to increase compensation significantly, for it is likely they are getting a great deal for the investment.

4. Before initiating any new program, consider this question: Who's going to do the work that is required to implement this properly?

It is easy to sit in the office and envision new programs and policies—and many of these may have merit—but at what cost, and from whose resources will that expense be paid? Whoever will be responsible for implementation may need to have something else removed from their responsibilities before adding anything new. Educators cannot simply be expected to continually add to their to-do list; leaders must be willing to relieve them of some existing duties each time a new program or initiative is considered.

5. Find creative ways to give time back to the staff.

One high school principal, a former math teacher, accomplished this by teaching each Algebra I section in the school for one week each year. This built trust on a variety of levels; the principal had the opportunity to come to know the students, he modeled for teachers that he was willing to take uncommon steps to stay in touch with their work, and—at least for those who were relieved of their duties for a period each day—they were given the gift of time.

Another approach is demonstrated by school administrators who take over a teacher's instructional or supervisory duties (recess, lunch, study hall). Leaders who adopt this strategy, for even a short period of time, build deeper levels of trust by modeling collaboration and a supportive approach to the staff.

These are not new ideas; almost any teaching staff in the country would come up with a similar list if asked how their leader could better show respect for their efforts. Many of these staff members are aspiring administrators themselves—just as many current administrators have entered the profession from the teaching ranks. So, why is it that suggestions such as these seem novel? Why is it that some school leaders, who spent years in the classroom before heading into the office, need to be encouraged to employ these strategies? Quite simply, it appears they have forgotten where they came from.

It may be that developing lengthy agendas, calling others to attend, and filling the day with committees and task forces provides a false sense of accomplishment for some leaders. Confident leaders have no need for this; they are comfortable with their role as leader, with a healthy ego that doesn't require the reinforcement that some gain from facilitating a meeting, no matter how repetitive or unworthy the agenda. Reflective leaders remember how stressful it is to rush from the classroom to the faculty meeting, and they seek to reduce that stress and honor the work their teachers do by giving them more time to do it.

BUILDING TRUST THROUGH
PROFESSIONAL DEVELOPMENT

Another significant area that provides unique opportunities for leaders to demonstrate trust is through professional development planning. Each year, school administrators are challenged to develop meaningful programming for staff that addresses the wide variation of needs across the district. These plans typically include a combination of in-service days, early release, or late arrival hours and individual or group learning opportunities.

District-level and school-level leaders have choices in how they plan these opportunities and who will have a say as to what is offered. Minimizing teacher voice in this planning is a surefire strategy for damaging the relationship between leaders and staff, whereas involving teachers in the development and execution of professional learning is an engaging and energizing way to foster trust at all levels of the school. The planning should be collaborative, with input from teacher representatives at the very least, if not from each teacher in the district, in order to get the buy-in necessary to make each experience worthwhile.

A common mistake in professional development planning is assuming that the "experts" reside elsewhere. Leaders who recognize the strengths and capabilities of their own staff can raise the level of trust in their school by asking employees to share their own expertise or explore timely topics with one another. Often, districts bring in costly presenters who provide a one-shot learning opportunity, impacting instruction in the school for a short period of time. Capitalizing on local expertise is not only less expensive, it is more accessible and can have a longer impact as the area of focus is revisited over time.

Several school districts that have been recognized for effectiveness and efficiency have employed strategies that engage staff in the identification, planning, and presenting of staff learning activities such as those identified here:

1. Collect teacher input.

This can be done through a survey, most easily, or through discussion groups within each grade level or learning area team, with feedback provided to those responsible for planning professional development activities. If there are timely changes that will likely bring about the need for staff learning (such as new legislation around standards-based assessments or the implementation of new instructional technology), the administration should identify those changes up front and seek input regarding the need for professional development that addresses the identified needs.

2. Host "unconferences" or "ed camps."

There are a wide range of ideas for how these clinics are run, but the general idea is that staff come to the day with their own ideas for what they'd like to learn or share. Using any number of methods for collecting those ideas, from collaborative digital documents to old-fashioned newsprint and markers, teachers add their ideas to the list and as many ideas as possible are assigned to different locations throughout the building. Some of the rooms are simply a place for teachers to explore a specific topic, while others may have an individual teacher or group of teachers who have volunteered to share their expertise on a stated topic.

Districts that have implemented days like this report a high degree of teacher satisfaction and engagement at virtually no expense to the district. The workshops can be centered around a predetermined theme (e.g., digital citizenship, social-emotional learning, equity), or follow the more extreme format of an "unconference" with no unifying topic, which makes for an exciting day and provides teachers with even more say into what their learning will involve.

3. Partner with neighboring districts.

To further expand the knowledge base for local presenters, schools should consider joining forces with a neighboring district. Teachers love learning from one another, and what may be common practice in one school could be just what teachers need to consider in the school next door. Unconferences and ed camps provide a great structure for collaborating with a neighbor and can lead to lasting partnerships that benefit both schools well into the future.

4. Set up a "Local U."

Many teachers enjoy taking graduate courses throughout their careers, which is beneficial to the school, but also costly and, often, not as mission-focused as the district may prefer. Rather than having teachers enrolling in a wide variety of graduate classes at significant expense, administrators might consider allowing instructors within the district to teach meaningful, mission-focused courses that are open to educators in each school.

This can be done by asking potential instructors to submit course proposals that align with the demands of a graduate course. The instructor is paid a stipend for each course based on the number of enrollees, saving the district from reimbursing teachers for taking a course through the university. Of course, these credits will not count toward an advanced degree, but they could count toward recertification units for participants. Districts may also choose to recognize completion of these courses for advancement on the salary scale, which is attractive to many teachers who have no intention of leaving the district for other positions.

By aligning the courses offered with the needs identified by the staff and the school's mission, the district ensures a more cohesive approach to professional development and builds collegiality and expertise within the staff.

5. Work with a community partner to grant scholarships.

Many districts have parent-teacher organizations or education foundations that strive to support the district in meaningful ways. One way to accomplish this is by forming a partnership with the local foundation to provide professional development scholarships that allow staff members to attend conferences outside the district.

In one district that has adopted this approach, the foundation and the district have agreed that the focus of this learning should be on innovative instruction. Teachers submit proposals for attendance at conferences of this nature, with an understanding they will bring learning back to share with others in the school. This format provides teachers opportunities that would not be available through the annual budget. Excitement has grown throughout the district each passing year as scholarships are announced and colleagues head off to their all-expenses-paid experience.

Upon returning from their trips, teachers present a report to the foundation, including how they will share their learning with their colleagues. The collegiality that is developed between administration, teachers, and the foundation deepens the trust that permeates the district, giving teachers a sense of validation and appreciation that might otherwise go unnoticed.

Demonstrating respect for employee time and expertise should be among the easiest, most visible ways for school leaders to build trust. Leaders should capitalize on every possible opportunity to give time back to the staff by minimizing meeting time, limiting office-generated initiatives, and engaging staff in decisions about professional development.

Shared leadership requires true confidence and a lack of focus on oneself. Only the most competent, trusting leaders will be able to pull it off. Developing that confidence and maturity should be a personal goal for all school leaders, as attainment will result in a level of trust within the organization that will otherwise be out of reach.

Chapter 7

Management at the Core of Leadership

> *Good managers don't always make effective leaders, but the most effective leaders are consistently good managers.*

Imagine sitting in the first row of the balcony in an ornate music hall, anticipating the beginning of a symphony concert. Approximately 100 musicians are seated in organized fashion on the stage, arranging their sheet music and tuning their instruments in what momentarily sounds like a cacophony of confusion. Strings, woodwinds, percussion, and brass—each instrument lends its own unique sound to the preparatory dissonance of the moment.

The conductor steps to the podium and, with a few taps of the baton, brings the group to silence and attention. All eyes are on the conductor, who raises the baton and, through one quick movement after another, elicits from this vast array of individual instruments a rich, harmonious sound that exemplifies collaboration toward a unified goal: perfection in performance of the piece at hand.

Orchestras parallel schools in many ways. The conductor personifies leadership, facilitating the adoption of a vision and mission for the symphony, bringing together the necessary performers, arranging them in a logical format, helping them interpret their individual pieces, and fusing each contribution to the framework that results in the desired outcome. To be most effective, the conductor must possess a tremendous amount of technical knowledge of music history, composition, and transposition, along with interpretive and performance skills, creativity, presence, and an ability to communicate—often in multiple languages.

The analogy to the school leader is strong, most likely because leadership is leadership, whether it's conducting an orchestra, coaching a soccer team, operating a restaurant, or running a school, and the most effective leaders must consistently demonstrate a vast array of skills similar to those embodied by the conductor.

MANAGING TO LEAD

Over the past few decades, *management* and *leadership* have been separated from one another in the minds of many constituents, and management has become an underappreciated skill set in many circles. When discussing the qualities of leadership with practicing and aspiring principals, it is no longer surprising to hear the disdain expressed for the term "management." It seems that in recent decades, educators have been conditioned to bemoan the actions of managers, promoting the more esoteric virtues of leadership as "good" and the mundane tasks of management as "bad."

While many have come to view management as an arcane set of skills and actions that are oppressive and constraining on the organization and any individuals in it, leadership has been elevated to a lofty position in which vision and collaboration raise the organization to new heights. Graduate students and employees in general have been led to believe that a person is either a leader or they are a manager. This is, of course, fallacy. The most effective leaders are recognized as such because they possess both management and leadership skills, rather than one or the other.

In truth, while good managers do not always make effective leaders, the most effective leaders are always good managers, for management is a core competency of leadership. The symphony conductor is a prime example. While the best conductors have a unique vision and ability to interpret music and meld hundreds of individual performances into one coordinated melody, they will not accomplish that feat without sound managerial skills that ask and answer organizational questions such as:

- Which instruments are needed and how many of each?
- How will they be arranged on the stage?
- How much room is needed between varying instruments?

Imagine an orchestra being led by a conductor with poor management skills; the bass player is drowning out the flutist, the trumpet player can't see the conductor, and there isn't enough sheet music for each of the cellists to have their own copy. The result may be a decent rendition of the composition, but it will not be the artful presentation that comes only from a blend of both management and leadership. Just as the conductor who cannot manage is more likely to produce a disjointed concerto, so too will a disorganized school leader reduce the likelihood that the school will advance toward its mission.

EXECUTIVE FUNCTIONING

As discussed throughout this text, and in a vast number of journals, textbooks, and dissertations dedicated to leadership studies, the most effective leaders possess a wide range of skills. While that list can become quite extensive, it can be argued that the majority of those skills fit quite easily within the definition of "executive functioning," those mental and emotional processes by which individuals plan, focus, multi-task, and regulate responses to stimuli.

Studying executive functioning is big business in the United States. Schools hire numerous staff to identify deficiencies and develop executive functioning skills in students, while private businesses contract with executive functioning coaches to hone the skills of current and potential leaders. The work is not so robust in the educational sector, unfortunately. While there is no lack of need, local school budgets seldom allow for the executive coaching that would help many school leaders avoid the pitfalls that land them on the evening news or, worse, in the market for a new job.

Executive function checklists typically consist of anywhere from six to twelve skills, but almost all of them include:

1. planning and prioritizing
2. task initiation
3. organization
4. working memory
5. impulse control
6. emotional control
7. flexible thinking
8. self-monitoring

To be an effective *manager*, one must demonstrate items 1 through 4 consistently. With these skills in their personal toolbox, good managers can keep an organization afloat, completing necessary day-to-day tasks and giving others confidence that the school is staying on course toward its mission, with some limited potential for improvement.

To be an effective *leader*, however, one must demonstrate not only the core management skills of planning, prioritizing, task initiation, organization, and working memory, but also the higher-order skills of impulse control, emotional control, flexibility, and self-monitoring. In this way, management

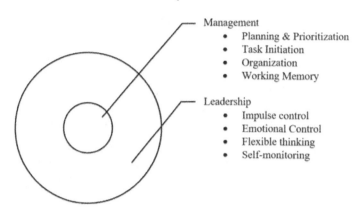

Figure 7.1   Concentric Circles of Management and Leadership. *Sources*: Author created.

skills and leadership skills don't exist in conflict with one another—rather, management is a core component of effective leadership.

As illustrated in figure 7.1, truly effective leaders possess the ability to manage while leading. Without this core competency, the leader will face significant challenges building trust, as disorganization leads to tasks being overlooked, sloppily completed, or poorly arranged. When disorganization impacts individuals or groups in the school—such as when a reimbursement request isn't processed, a course approval form is misplaced, or buses aren't scheduled for a field trip—confidence and trust in the leader are diminished.

Stated differently, management tasks are the low-hanging fruit of leadership; they provide ripe opportunities for leaders to demonstrate competence. When management tasks are completed with efficiency, the leader models for the staff how business should be conducted, setting the bar for staff performance. When left unattended, this low-level fruit quickly spoils, and assumption of leadership incompetence develops among the staff.

Consider the high school principal who once said, "You've got to get the graduation ceremony right. For many people in attendance, it will be their only direct exposure to your school." At his rural school, graduation was a first-class celebration unlike any other in the community's list of annual events. Year after year, the ceremony received rave reviews from all constituents, raising the esteem with which the school and the school's leaders were viewed by the public.

Without the attention to detail and organization given to the event, the school could look sloppy, unprofessional, and careless. Misspelling student names in the graduation program, miscounting the number of chairs needed for the graduates or forgetting to do a sound check on the microphones are surefire ways to bring about justified criticisms of the school. They are also easy items to take care of with a focus on core management skills.

Managing without Leading

It is not enough to manage, though. About school administrators who seldom venture outside the management core, it is often said, "There's just no vision for where we're headed or how we'll get there," or "He's just a bean counter." The bells ring on time, report cards are distributed as scheduled, and school assemblies come off without a hitch—none of which should go unacknowledged—but the efficiency with which those tasks are completed may come at the expense of the relationships necessary to drive the school toward greater performance.

Leading without Managing

Conversely, school administrators who operate solely in the outer ring of the leadership sphere, with little ability to manage, are criticized as well. About these leaders, critics frequently say, "She's a great 'big picture' person, but she can't get anything done." Tasks are overlooked, items are misplaced, and those impacted are left feeling unappreciated or disenfranchised. The school may have a well-crafted mission statement, but the inability to oversee basic management of the school hinders any opportunities for orderly, coordinated improvement.

Where there is management without leadership, the organization lacks direction; where there is leadership without management, there is waste, missed opportunity, and duplication of effort. The school leader is much like the maestro, with dozens of employees that each bring to the school varying skills that contribute to the overall performance of the school. While some constituents yearn for leaders who display the soft skills of leadership, others appreciate leaders who make sure the buses run on time. When the leader demonstrates the ability to manage *and* lead, fans of both styles will be more likely to join the effort to move the organization forward.

STRENGTHENING THE CORE

There is little tolerance for leaders who lack management skills, and school administrators have myriad opportunities to hone those skills each day. The most effective leaders make it look easy. For the rest, management competencies are not as clearly demonstrated, and an intentional approach to tackling task-oriented opportunities is necessary. Fortunately, while the higher-order skills of leadership may take years to develop, core competencies in management can be markedly improved in a short timespan with focused effort that may include:

1. Recognizing the importance of management.

Leaders must avoid buying into the "management is bad" theory of leadership. This is the first step to ensuring that details are not missed—something that will be appreciated by many in the organization, and a low bar that should not provide a significant hurdle for even the most inexperienced leader.

2. Conducting an honest self-assessment of management skills.

One way for leaders to better understand their own performance in this area is to ask others to answer the following questions:

- Do I appear organized, or are meetings and tasks that are my obligation often confusing, behind schedule, or completed at the last minute?
- Do I present information in an orderly, understandable fashion?
- Do events and tasks for which I have primary responsibility typically run well, or are there often last-minute troubleshooting challenges that must be addressed?

Leaders who are often harried and stressed just prior to meetings, scurrying to put together information or organize materials likely could make some improvements in this area.

3. Not reinventing the wheel.

The ability to avoid making the same mistakes over and over again is a key management skill. Because many school events occur annually, from developing the master schedule to reviewing the student handbook, a challenge that is faced one year is often replicated when the task is repeated twelve months later. Creating annual checklists to guide the school through recurring events allows leaders to be better prepared to handle the cyclical tasks of the school year.

On a similar front, creating an annual calendar with deadlines by which certain tasks are to be completed will help less organized leaders avoid oversights and missteps. Few administrative actions are met with more disdain than the last-minute notice of an upcoming due date for items such as budget submissions or student award nominations. An annual calendar will provide for a more orderly year on all fronts.

4. Asking for help.

The best leaders are strong managers, or they recognize that weakness in themselves and enlist the assistance of others to take care of management tasks that may otherwise be overlooked (another effective management strategy). A competent administrative assistant or an organized member of the leadership team may be counted on to strengthen the leader's performance and leave time for the higher-order tasks of leadership.

School leadership is messy. Varied perspectives, opinions, and philosophies—not to mention political beliefs—can turn the simplest of topics into a tempestuous public conflict. It is unlikely every school day will feel like a well-conducted symphony, but with recognition that management is an essential component of effective leadership, administrators can set the stage for school improvement in an organized and efficient manner.

Chapter 8

Collaborative Trust

A trusting leader is a trusted leader.

Much has been said and written about collaborative leadership in recent years, and yet, in courses preparing future school leaders for the role of principal, director, and superintendent, many graduate students claim it still does not exist to the level they would like to see in their schools. They share their perspectives of school leaders making decisions in isolation, withholding information from staff, and micromanaging situations.

This is disheartening to hear, especially when one considers that most current school leaders were trained in the same programs that are preparing future school leaders. Despite the focus on shared leadership strategies in graduate courses, students believe some leaders struggle to employ these strategies in real time.

Why is this the case? What happens between that time when an aspiring leader articulately espouses the need for shared leadership while enrolled in graduate school and the time when they become the leader accused of the same authoritarianism that they so passionately condemned?

One theory is that many aspiring leaders, not unlike many employees, are advocates for shared leadership during times when they are not the ultimate decision-maker, struggling for their voice to be heard. In those moments, the call for shared leadership is personally beneficial. Without it, the individual feels unheard, voiceless, and left out of the decision-making process. Contrarily, when one becomes the leader, they no longer have to worry about their voice being heard; they easily lose sight of the need for shared leadership and fall into the same autocratic trappings that have led to the demise of many otherwise competent leaders.

Shared leadership is a necessary strategy of successful people-oriented organizations as large and complex as schools. The demands of leadership positions make it nearly impossible for one person to provide effective leadership in all of the areas for which they are responsible. Instruction, curriculum, finance, personnel, student management, public relations, transportation, nutrition, assessment, accountability—the list goes on and on, and the layers of the organization go deeper and deeper. Collaboration not only fosters trust between the leader and constituents but also makes the job of school leadership more manageable.

TRUSTING OTHERS TO MAKE A GOOD IDEA BETTER

One principal in a fast-growing, suburban school was concerned that the "small school" feel was being lost as enrollment increased by nearly 50 percent in just a few years. Determined to ensure students were known by the staff and did not fall through the cracks, the principal considered implementing a teaming model for the youngest students in which four teachers would share eighty students and be provided common planning time and professional learning opportunities. The teachers would be assigned classrooms in close proximity to one another to promote informal and formal interactions with students and one another.

The principal knew better than to simply spring this idea on teachers, for the model in its purest form would require reassigning courses and classrooms for a fair number of staff members. Rather than present the idea as a fait accompli, the principal asked the leadership team to identify concerns that were arising due to the school's growth. Staff members were invited to add to the list and to begin sharing ideas for addressing the concerns. It did not take long for teachers to identify the same challenges and suggest the same types of solutions the principal had considered, and a group of teachers volunteered to explore the concept of teaming.

Over the course of several months, with minimal input (but firm support) from the principal, the group developed a proposal that resulted in the adoption of a team model for students in the ninth grade. While many of their ideas ran parallel to those of the principal, the teachers' proximity to students and the day-to-day operations that impact student and faculty life allowed them to develop a more robust model than the principal would have created on his own.

Teachers led the restructuring effort, sharing their ideas with colleagues and providing the rationale for the change. The discussions around reassignment of courses and classrooms went much more smoothly than they might have had the idea come directly from the principal's office, with colleagues supporting one another through the changes. By the opening of school in the fall, teachers had been reassigned and relocated as necessary to give the experiment its best chance for success.

Had the principal taken on this effort with a top-down mandate or initiated the conversation with a proposed solution to a problem that had yet to be agreed upon, the effort would likely have been met with opposition or, at the very least, trepidation. Instead, by trusting the faculty to understand the challenges being faced, and by having confidence that they may come up with even better solutions to those challenges, the principal created an environment in which the staff took ownership of the proposal, explained the rationale to their colleagues, and implemented a program in the best interest of students.

By not caring who got the credit, the principal demonstrated self-confidence and accomplished something significant for kids, recognizing that it's not important whose ideas are adopted as part of the overall solution; what's important is the difference those ideas make in the lives of students.

The principal's work in this example began well before the implementation of the team format; it began by hiring teachers who had experience with teaming or those that indicated a desire to collaborate on a more meaningful level. The groundwork for this effort was laid in the recruitment and hiring of staff whose professional goals matched those of the school, so that when the time came for action, the right people were present to move the organization forward.

COMMITTEES AREN'T ALWAYS THE ANSWER

When asked to describe how they will provide teacher and student voice in the school, many aspiring school leaders immediately talk about the formation of committees and working groups tasked with specific (or, in the worst cases, vague) responsibilities. The Attendance Committee, the School Climate Team, the Scheduling Task Force; schools are bursting at the seams with groups that, on the surface, appear to have responsibility for meaningful school structures and protocols—even schools where staff members feel they have no real voice.

While these working groups are necessary in many situations, it is important to recognize that shared leadership requires much more than creating committees and task forces that submit reports. True shared leadership comes only when individuals and groups other than the leader feel empowered to do the work and influence change.

BUILDING COLLABORATION

In most schools, it is not the lack of shared leadership structures that prevent staff and students from feeling they have a voice—it is the lack of a collaborative culture in the building. As has been pointed out throughout this text, that culture is developed through the fostering of trusting relationships that allow people to feel heard, valued, and respected each day they come to school. Leaders intent on creating and fostering a culture of authentic collaboration would do well to consider a variety of strategies to ensure staff members trust the sincerity of those intentions:

1. Recognize the importance of informal dialogue.

Culture, not structure, is the key to shared leadership in any organization. All the structures and protocols that allow "School A" to arrive at a place of collaboration may exist down the road in "School B" where ineffective leadership results in cynicism and failed initiatives. The difference? School A has an administrator who engenders trust that shared decisions will be made and implemented, while School B is led by an individual who puts all the right teams in place but has not done the interpersonal work necessary to convince staff that they are trusted to share their voice.

A leader who is truly interested in shared leadership demonstrates interest in what others are thinking—not just in the formal settings of committee work, but also in informal interactions with constituents throughout the school. A principal who takes the time to drop in on teachers as they are working in their classrooms to ask their opinions on a timely topic will find teachers more willing to share and trust that their opinions matter. The follow-up to those conversations is important, too. Confidential conversations must be honored. Teachers need to know they are safe to share their ideas without being scorned by others if their opinion is not popular.

2. Foster a culture of continual improvement.

Many schools struggle to overcome the "things are fine as they are" attitude, especially schools that are consistently recognized for high performance. In such settings, and even in those where student performance struggles to meet articulated standards, it is critical for the leader to honor the work that has been done while helping the staff recognize the importance of continual improvement.

Leaders will find constituents much more likely to accept the need to evolve if they are also given a little praise at the same time. Pointing out that the school has been very effective at meeting student needs over the past few years, but those needs are changing, and the challenge will be to continue to lead in the coming years, will be more effective than saying "We aren't good enough."

3. Stay focused on the shared mission.

As will be discussed in chapter 16, the most effective schools are those in which a shared mission is developed and embraced throughout the organization. Where a common mission does not exist, there is no clear direction. With a clear mission, and consistent focus on that mission, staff have faith that their work is in alignment throughout the school, and leaders are confident that meaningful forward progress is being made, rather than sidetracking.

Each working group, from the short-term task force to the long-standing committee, must be cognizant of their role in promoting the mission. With clearly delineated areas of responsibility, well-defined work products, and common understanding of how their work fits into the larger construct of the school, these groups are more likely to generate ideas and proposals that will win the support of the school leadership and constituents.

4. Don't "overcommittee."

Well-meaning school leaders often move directly to form a new committee each time they are faced with a challenging situation. Confusion between buses, private vehicles, and walkers during the morning drop-off time? Set up a Morning Drop-Off Committee. Students struggling to get from class to class on time? Set up a Bell Schedule Review Committee. Teachers having a difficult time finding a parking spot in the morning? Set up a Parking Lot Oversight Committee.

This isn't always the best response, though. It is important to delineate between times when constituents want problems fixed, times when they want their ideas considered as part of the solution, and times when they just want to voice their concern. The formation of committees doesn't effectively address two of these three scenarios. Being an astute listener and understanding what is called for in each situation is the first step toward creating a collaborative culture.

When faced with concerns from a constituent, the leader must provide the air-time necessary for their colleague, student, or community member to fully articulate their thoughts. Asking follow-up questions, including, "Do you have a suggestion for how we should address this?" demonstrates empathy and gives the complainant a sense that their concern will be taken seriously.

There are a wide range of responses to be considered between dismissing the complaint out of hand and forming a committee to study the problem. The collaborative leader recognizes that not every situation demands a community response. For the majority of staff, students, and parents, it is their personal relationship with the leader—not their participation on a task force—that provides the greatest sense of collaboration.

5. Be clear about roles and responsibilities.

When it is necessary to have working groups, it is vital that the group understands its role in the decision-making process. Will the group have the authority to make decisions, or will they be advisory to the administration? Will decisions be made by consensus, majority rule, or negotiation? The formation of committees can be an effective way to promote collaboration in the school, but lack of clarity around the committee's working rules and level of responsibility will lead to frustration and distrust. Agreeing to those parameters from the outset gives participants the confidence necessary to work more effectively as part of the team.

6. Don't force, nor discourage, participation.

Effective leaders must come to know the staff in a way that allows them to engage each member in a manner that is comfortable, yet encourages them to expand their influence at the school. Some teachers will say, "I don't want to be involved in all those decisions; I just want to close my door and teach." As long as the instruction they are providing is of a high caliber, that may be an acceptable approach. However, it will be important for the leader to find ways to engage that individual in areas that may strike a chord, lest they become too isolated and, unbeknownst to others, disenfranchised in the school.

Others will want to take on too much, volunteering for every committee or task force that comes along. Helping these enthusiastic employees focus their energies and provide space for others to participate is a tenuous proposition at times. Leaders must encourage them to share the load with others, possibly even setting up parameters that gently, but clearly, suggest a wider sharing of responsibilities throughout the school.

7. Share relevant data and let the group decide.

One of the most effective strategies for fostering trust throughout the school is to let ideas formulate from the grassroots—from teachers, staff, and students. On the professional level, this demonstrates trust in the educators working at the school—and they deserve that trust; for the most part, they are experienced, educated, compassionate individuals. When faced with a difficult decision, or when inspired to try a different approach, a trusting, confident leader may simply need to share with the staff the data and research that suggest a change and allow the staff to define the need and develop solutions organically.

As with the principal who led the staff to a team-based approach earlier in this chapter, it is likely the staff will develop ideas that are at least as good as those the leader would have developed alone. Even better, those ideas will come with a built-in degree of buy-in, rather than a healthy dose of skepticism. This approach deepens the level of trust the leader has in the staff as they produce ideas and solutions that exceed the leader's individual thoughts. Similarly, the group's trust in the leader will grow as they gain confidence that their opinion matters in sight of the leader relying more and more on the wisdom of the group.

8. Allow staff to identify areas in which they would like to have a voice.

Many schools have implemented "genius hour" or "passion projects" that allow students and staff opportunities to self-select areas in which they would like to expand their learning. These strategies are effective for many different reasons, but mostly because they provide choice—a critical characteristic of trust-filled schools. Teachers should be encouraged to explore interests that align with the school's mission, and to present their proposals for integrating those interests into the learning continuum. When instructors are passionate about what they are teaching, they are more likely to create engaging lessons that stimulate learning.

COLLABORATING WHEN IT COUNTS

The COVID-19 pandemic of 2020–2022 provided school leaders with unparalleled challenges. Instead of planning for the typical school year, superintendents and principals found themselves embroiled in discussions about transmission rates, social distancing, trajectory of exhalations, and air-exchange systems, not to mention student and staff home Internet access, synchronous versus asynchronous teaching, remote learning platforms, and legal concerns about the recording of online classes.

The rapidly evolving information from public health experts, facilities managers, and transportation officials, along with the daily flooding of in-boxes from technology providers and instructional consultants, provided school leaders with an overload of information to sort through as they determined how best to provide meaningful instruction while keeping students and staff safe. In those schools that moved most effectively into what became known as "pandemic instruction mode," school communities participated in unprecedented collaborative decision-making efforts.

School personnel from nurses and custodians to teachers and social workers sat alongside principals, superintendents, special educators, and curriculum directors to develop comprehensive plans that addressed everything from bus protocols to personal hygiene to virtual meeting etiquette. This collaboration and communication created a sense of community and cohesiveness that allowed the best run schools to develop comprehensive plans focused first on health and wellness and second on effective instruction.

One of the most important lessons to be learned by school leaders from COVID-19 was the effectiveness of collaborative decision-making. Leaders don't need to have all the answers, but they do need to know who they can rely upon to provide the most accurate information in each situation.

No leader survived making decisions in isolation during the pandemic—from the highest levels of government to local schools. The structures and learnings from the COVID-19 pandemic will remain with those who lived through it for many years. Future leaders will do well to reflect on those learnings to provide collaborative structures in their schools, even if the task at hand is not addressing a worldwide health crisis.

Shared leadership in a culture of collaboration is a characteristic of schools operating at the highest level of organizational and individual trust. The trusting leader becomes the trusted leader by effectively providing for constituent voice, understanding when others simply need to be heard, when they need to be involved in decision-making, and when they just want their problems solved. Listening, seeking clarification, and knowing where to go for answers are the seminal steps in building that collaborative culture.

Part III

FOSTERING TRUST
WITH STUDENTS

Chapter 9

Leading for All

Assuming equity exists at school is the surest sign that it doesn't.

Many Americans likely fail to realize that the nation's public schools were founded on the belief that an educated citizenry would be less likely to fall prey to the temptations of Satan. In 1642, *The Massachusetts School Law* instructed parents to educate their children in the English language. This was America's first legislation regarding compulsory schooling. The law was poorly enforced and, in 1647, the Commonwealth passed the *Old Deluder Satan Act*, stating that each individual should be able to read and interpret the Bible for themselves, placing the responsibility of educating children on the community.

These puritanical laws were easily adopted with little opposition due to the homogeneous composition of the communities in which they were introduced. The United States was not yet the diverse land it has become since the Revolution. As our diversity as a nation has grown, so has the expectation that, just as every citizen has a voice through the democratic processes of our government, so, too, must all students be afforded equitable access to educational opportunities.

EQUITY

It is crucial for school leaders to understand what equity is and how it differs from equality. While *equality* promotes fairness by treating everyone the same, *equity* recognizes the differences in individuals and treats them differently based on need. Where equality is measured by inputs, that is, providing everyone the same access to the same resources, equity is concerned with outputs, that is, providing each individual what is needed to reach a common standard. Equality asks, "How do we provide the same resources to everyone so they have an equal shot at success?" while equity asks, "How do we provide each person what they need to reach the goal?"

For some students, little if anything beyond the basic school programming is required to help them attain the standards the school sets for them. For others, the school realizes additional supports are needed for a wide range of challenges—academic, social-emotional, or physical to name those most often addressed through school programming.

There are many students for whom equity is a concern; students receiving services through special education or the Americans with Disabilities Act, students of color, gender fluid students, students living in poverty, students from nontraditional families, and students with a wide range of family or personal characteristics that set them apart in one way or another from the majority of their peers. Those backgrounds have significant impact on the level to which students access school programming each day.

While many students come to school well-fed, others rely on the school for basic nutrition. Where some are provided the resources and support to complete homework without difficulty, others may spend their time after school working, caring for family members, or cleaning up after yet another domestic disturbance in their home. Where some enjoy a school in which most of their teachers and classmates look like them, dress like them, and talk like them, others come to a place that is very different from their home, surrounded by classmates and teachers who speak a different language, wear different types of clothing, and have a much different life experience.

While overt acts of discrimination are infuriating and discouraging, many of the slights these students experience in schools and in larger society are less visible and require greater examination by all who believe in the democratic values on which the United States was founded.

Once leaders understand what equity is and why it is important for their school, they can begin the work of understanding why it doesn't exist in the school in as pervasive a manner as they might hope. That work begins at the individual level, and it is personal and difficult, for it begins with leaders recognizing the implicit bias with which they themselves operate. This is challenging work; few school leaders likely entered the profession believing that they held biases against individuals or groups who were different from them.

Accepting that individual and institutional biases are real and impactful is a deeply personal inflection point that is unlikely to occur without guidance from others with greater understanding of intercultural development. While there are plenty of books that can be read on this topic, it may be important for school leaders to engage the services of consultants who make use of personal inventories to help them better understand their own perspectives and how their beliefs and experiences create unintentional bias at the school.

As this work is completed at the individual level, leaders must be prepared to bring the entire staff into the discussion, with personal and school-wide examination of implicit and explicit bias. This can be gut-wrenching work. Most educators are "good people" who will want to declare, "I'm not biased! I love all my students and care about them regardless of their background." And it is likely that they believe that and try to live it each day. Still, understanding that bias does not just reveal itself through overt acts, but also in the ways in which schools craft policies that inadvertently impact students differently, is an important concept for school leaders to grasp.

Real-World Applications

Student restrooms are one area where discussion and debate have blossomed in recent years, as more students are coming forward at a younger age to share their experiences as transgender or nonbinary individuals. Being forced to use gender-specific bathrooms can be a significant concern for both the transgender student and cisgender students who don't yet understand gender fluidity, non-binarism, or gender identity.

When a transgender student indicates discomfort using the bathroom expected of them either because of their stated gender identity or because of the gender assigned to them at birth, schools often make the well-intentioned mistake of offering the use of a gender-neutral bathroom, such as one in the nurse's office, or one next to the principal's office, or one in the faculty workroom.

Those options, while intended to provide privacy and relieve the student of the anxiety associated with using the larger bathrooms, set the student apart and identify them in a way that many underrepresented students find objectionable. A better option is to provide *all* students with the option to use a private bathroom, possibly designating a bathroom in each area of the school as gender-neutral. By making this adjustment, any students who find it preferable or more convenient to use such a room may do so, which begins to remove the stigma of the bathroom being only for those who are gender fluid.

Examples abound on this topic, even in the most progressive schools. In one district where English Language Learner (ELL) and transgender student enrollment had grown exponentially in the previous decade, school leaders had engaged in the work of understanding implicit bias and addressing equity throughout the school for several years. Surveys within the district indicated that staff felt they were on top of this issue and addressing concerns with great compassion.

More than two years after beginning the work, the school was contacted by a parent who said, "I logged into our child's information portal and was entering our family data, and it only has one line for 'mother's name' and another for 'father's name,' and we're a two-mom family. Can something be done about that?" Despite all the work that had been done and the attention that had been given to eradicating discriminatory practices from the schools, examples still existed where implicit bias had a negative impact on the day-to-day experiences of various constituents.

In this case, the bias was easily addressed with a simple call to the technology department, resulting in a change on the student information screen. Not all missteps are as easy to correct but fixing some of these "broken windows" may indicate the goodwill necessary for schools to deal with more intense concerns in proactive, rather than defensive, fashion.

Acknowledge the Need for Equity

School leaders must recognize and publicly declare equity to be a core focus of the school's work each year, regardless of whether they work in a large school with a great deal of diversity or a small school where it seems everyone is related to one another. The fact is the world is a diverse place. It is that world for which all students should be prepared, and acceptance of inequity in even the most remote locations contributes to inequity wherever those students may go.

One of the most challenging aspects of equity work is the political and emotional nature of the public response, regardless of who the leaders are who are promoting the effort. The work takes courage, clear communication, and constant maintenance of effort if it is to bring about meaningful and sustainable change for the school and, eventually, the community at large.

Tackling Equity Where It Matters

Navigating school-wide or district-wide equity programming requires thoughtful planning and intent. Many schools have taken meaningful steps toward greater equity by employing a range of strategies that are shared here:

1. Adopt a core value, with a clearly stated annual goal, focused on equity.

In chapter 16, the importance of a concisely stated mission statement will be discussed as a critical step for schools to take in order to define what it is they stand for and where they hope to go. One major component of that mission statement should be focused on issues of equity, with at least one annual goal designed to promote equity throughout the school. This statement should be adopted by the school board after a public presentation and discussion and then shared widely through the normal communications platforms for the district.

Schools that publicly declare their focus and goals each year and hold themselves accountable through public reporting of measurable data build greater trust in the community. The public can be assured school leaders are not merely talking a good game but taking intentional steps toward meeting stated goals. School leaders should work at the building level to identify areas of need and provide the school board with suggested language for annual goals and actionable items to be completed each year, recognizing that this work never ends but continues to evolve and demand daily attention.

2. Engage the community in the work.

Most schools will have no problem finding passionate members of the community to assist in this work. While chapter 8 reminded school leaders to be cautious about forming too many committees to address items that might be handled in more efficient manners, equity is one area of focus that requires input from a broad range of constituents. Inviting parents, students, staff, and community members to participate in a thoughtful, ongoing review and planning process with regular public sharing of information through the district website, social media apps, and other platforms will keep this work at the forefront of the school's annual effort.

Engaging the right people in this work is a balancing act. Certainly, any task force should be comprised of individuals who are representative of the community. At the same time, schools have been criticized for expecting members of an underrepresented group to be responsible for enlightening the majority about bias and discrimination. A committee focused on equity should be composed neither only of members of the majority community nor only of members of the minority community. The group should be a model for dialogue between and among various constituent groups, where the advantaged come to listen, first, and collaboratively problem-solve second.

3. Engage experienced professionals.

While many educators care passionately about issues of diversity, equity, and inclusion, these are not core components of teacher training at the undergraduate level, nor has the work been germane to leadership training courses for a significant period of time. Even if it were, the complexity of the work and the critical and changing nature of getting it right may require input from consultants or other professionals who, unlike school leaders, do not have responsibility for dozens of other projects and programs. These individuals can help guide the school's work in ways that more closely align with the perspectives of those the school is trying to serve.

4. Conduct an equity audit.

While every school leader should be able to identify and eliminate covert acts of discrimination, many unintentional biases are less visible. Policies and practices at the school may target certain populations; programming that has existed for decades may not be accessible to all; curriculum and instructional materials may ignore the experiences and voices of various members of the school population. Some of the more visible yet long-perpetuated challenges schools have uncovered when conducting an audit focused on equity include:

- Extra-curricular programming that is too costly for individual students or requires personal transportation outside of school hours, thereby reducing access for some students.
- Classroom libraries, even at the youngest grade levels, filled with books with a dearth of characters from minority cultures and backgrounds.
- Curriculum that ignores the role bias and discrimination has played, and continues to play, in the United States and across the globe.
- Policies such as dress codes that target a specific population of students in an unbalanced way.

Reviewing curriculum, policies, and practices that impact student learning takes considerable effort. To do it well requires a great deal of human capital. School leaders who avoid this work do a disservice not only to students who may be marginalized but also to members of non-marginalized groups who miss out on opportunities to appreciate the differences found in others.

5. Develop recruitment, hiring, and onboarding practices that promote equity.

While student populations in many schools continue to diversify, teacher demographics have remained relatively stable since 1999, with white teachers comprising nearly 80 percent of the workforce as late as 2018.[1] Diverse faculty are even more difficult to find in rural districts further from metropolitan areas, despite the fact that many schools in those districts have experienced demographic shifts in the student population. While it has been shown that teachers of color help to close the achievement gap for students of color,[2] schools often struggle to hire and retain a diverse staff.

One of the specific tasks of the school's equity committee should be to explore the development of standardized hiring protocols that require training for all administrators and hiring team participants in best practices for recruiting, interviewing, and reviewing candidates. The importance of hiring and retaining the best teachers will be discussed in greater detail in chapter 10 but is worth previewing here.

Hiring and developing an expert staff is the single most important task of the school leader who intends to impact student learning and development in a significant way. Being intentional about the wording and placement of advertisements, understanding how to avoid interview bias, and prioritizing diversity in the hiring process will only serve to strengthen the school's ability to hire teachers with the best opportunity to engage all students.

Onboarding new hires through an engaging orientation process, connecting them with mentors who will enthusiastically support them and promote the school's mission, and providing them with professional development opportunities that are meaningful for their work are routine activities of the trust-building school leader.

6. Promote successes, declare challenges.

Schools that demonstrate significant progress in promoting diversity, equity, and inclusion have done so largely because of their willingness to be publicly accountable for that work. Websites, newsletters, and press releases are utilized not only to promote the school's successes but also to identify the challenges that must be confronted in order to promote equity. Setting up a webpage to share the work of the equity committee is an enjoyable task, providing an opportunity to reiterate the school's commitment to this work; more challenging is sending out a notice to the community that a disturbing incident has taken place that threatens inclusion.

In one district where this work had become a focus, a racial epithet was spray-painted on a structure not far from the schools. The school leader in this case had two options: (1) declare that it did not occur on school grounds and therefore did not require a response from the school, or (2) denounce the act and state support for members of the community (including staff and students) who identified with the target of the epithet. The leader opted for the second approach, which proved the best strategy for building trust as empathy grew for those who were targeted and the community identified a need to address the behavior.

Schools that have successfully embarked on this journey recognize that there is no endpoint for this work. Microcosms of the society, schools must continually evolve while recognizing that there are milestones that can be met along the way. Intentional, accountable effort is necessary to make those milestones more achievable.

NOTES

1. https://nces.ed.gov/programs/coe/indicator_clr.asp.
2. https://learningpolicyinstitute.org/press-release/teachers-color-high-demand -and-short-supply.

Chapter 10

Hiring for Kids

The most effective way to build trust with students is to provide them with expert instructors who care about them as individuals.

The importance of employing compassionate, highly competent professionals in every position in the school cannot be overstated; it is the most critical quality of a high-performing school, and attracting and retaining the best educators at all levels of the school organization is arguably the single most important job of the school leader. Teachers, support personnel, bus drivers, nutrition workers, every adult in the organization impacts the lives of the students with whom they interact, making implementation of a rigorous hiring and supervisory model the most significant work school leaders undertake each year.

More important than having the newest technology or the latest curriculum, schools must be filled with adults who care about students, can relate to students, and have moral authority—not authority granted by the position they hold, but authority they have developed through consistent modeling of integrity and empathy. When schools are staffed with professionals who exhibit these attributes, each student stands a better chance of receiving expert instruction and having at least one adult in the building on whom they can count and in whom they may confide or seek counsel.

In schools where staff lack moral authority and are more concerned with legislated authority (authority vested in them by the laws of the state and policies of the school board), it widens the chasms that often exist between adults and students, leaving many students feeling ostracized, disempowered, or invisible. The school leader has the ultimate responsibility for employing a staff with moral authority. From the recruiting and hiring process through orientation, support, and supervision, the leader must embrace the opportunity to shape the school's culture through its most impactful component—its people.

Often, school leaders assume they will have little impact on the personnel in the building because of the experienced composition of the staff. Leaders who resign themselves to the belief that attitudes and approaches in veteran staff cannot be changed start down the misdirected path of trying to improve the school only by tackling tasks such as revamping curriculum, restructuring daily schedules, or updating classroom technology.

These may be necessary activities, and some may result in improved performance, but the fact remains that the leader's greatest impact on student learning comes not from changing the bell schedule or selecting a new textbook, but from ensuring that each area of the school is staffed by adults who have adopted the school's vision for what is best for kids.

HIRING THE WRONG PEOPLE

While it is recognized that education is the ultimate people-oriented business, schools too often have the wrong people in the wrong positions in the organization. There are many reasons for this, from rushed hiring processes to limited applicant pools, and leaders must be careful to avoid these common pitfalls for hiring the wrong people:

- Because they have the right zip code.

It is tempting for schools to hire individuals because they live in the community—or a nearby community with a desirable reputation—inappropriately discriminating against others who may be more qualified but live in a less desirable location.

- Because "it's their turn."

Some educators are hired from within the school, having served as teachers' aides for a few years in order to become known to the staff. This happens frequently in leadership searches, as hiring teams employ "the devil you know" philosophy and promote the familiar face, rather than risk bringing in someone from outside the organization. While it is important to have some mechanisms in place for growing the school's talent pool from within, leaders must also be willing to look beyond the current staff to find the best candidates for their students.

- Because their family is known by the school.

Schools, rightly so, enjoy seeing their former students succeed. What better way to experience that than by hiring them to work at their alma mater or childhood school to keep local traditions and values alive? There is certainly something to be said for the sense of community and loyalty these former students bring to the job. However, when they are hired at the expense of someone who may bring better instructional practices or a fresh perspective to the organization, the school forfeits an opportunity to grow in exchange for doing what is comfortable.

- Because they look, act, and think exactly like others at the school.

Schools, like many organizations, do a great job of hiring people who represent exactly what the staff already believe themselves to be. Unfortunately, this stagnates growth and perpetuates current practices, rather than promoting new ideas and perspectives that may push the school to higher levels of performance. By seeking new team members that appear to think differently and are willing to take risks in new ways, schools can expand their impact on students and promote a healthy balance between respecting effective traditions and trying new approaches.

- Because they went to the "right" college.

Another downfall of hiring practices in some communities is the critical error of hiring individuals because they have a diploma from a highly regarded college or university. There are many reasons why individuals attend colleges where they do, and almost none of them has anything to do with a person's ability to engage students in daily lessons in which they may or may not have any natural interest.

School hiring teams often become enthralled by the transcript from a prestigious college and overlook the personal qualities necessary to maximize learning for students. A candidate who has overcome significant personal adversity may have many more of the skills and qualities necessary to forge meaningful relationships with students than the candidate who attended a highly regarded university. Selection committees must be cautious to consider the transcript as one marker in a much larger list of preferred qualities for each candidate.

HIRING THE RIGHT PEOPLE

On the flipside, there are many good reasons why the right people get hired in schools:

- Because their experiences and vision will help advance the school's mission.

School leaders are not the only educators who impact the school's mission. Indeed, the mission should be furthered each day by every member of the organization. Schools with a clear focus on continual improvement will view every hiring process as an opportunity to further that goal, and hiring educators who have demonstrated that same vision—or a strong desire to do so—will continually reenergize the school's efforts.

• Because they bring a different strength to the organization.

It is exciting to bring new professionals into the school and see how their influence grows over time. While it is important to orient new staff members to the school, it is also important to see where their strengths may help the school adopt new approaches that benefit students.

• Because they are willing to push the organization to think differently and be better.

Seeking candidates with different experiences provides a greater chance for existing staff members to learn from their new colleagues. Rather than simple indoctrination of the new staff, there is recognition that new hires may bring with them knowledge of a different way of doing things, and an authentic sharing of ideas and experiences among all staff members follows.

• Because they have a track record of success and perseverance.

Students benefit from working with adults who understand their challenges. While it is important that teachers have the knowledge and skills necessary to teach whatever curriculum has been assigned to them, it is critical that they have an ability to relate to the students they are teaching. When schools hire candidates who have real-life experiences analogous to those their students are facing, they increase the likelihood that healthy interpersonal relationships will be fostered throughout the school.

• Because they increase the diversity of the school's staff.

As was discussed in chapter 9, equity in hiring must be a major consideration in the selection process, so that employees represent not only the diversity of the student population but also the diversity students will experience when they leave their local community and venture further in the larger world. Effective hiring, then, must be recognized as a critical component of school improvement. Even in schools where teachers are hired and stay in their positions for decades, there are annual opportunities for bringing in new employees that should not be squandered.

HIRING STRATEGIES

Adoption of a rigorous and meaningful hiring process provides the framework for identifying the best candidates for the school. While interview teams, common question sheets, and rating systems are now standard practice to ensure an even playing field for all candidates, there are a few additional steps schools may take to provide a higher likelihood of the best outcome:

1. Engage others in the process.

This likely goes without saying, as it would be difficult to find a school that does not employ hiring teams in the selection of new teachers and administrators. However, it is important not only to include educators but also to provide the opportunity for parents and students to engage in the hiring process. The school's leadership team should be involved in setting up the selection committee to ensure the group is comprised of individuals who have embraced the school's mission and will provide the insight necessary to bring the best candidates on board.

At the middle school and high school level, it may be appropriate to include students on the interview team or even set up a team comprised solely of students. This is an effective way to gauge the candidate's ability to interact with students they will be working with if hired, and students always seem to share some valuable insights that are missed by the adults on the interview team. Having students provide a tour of the school is an additional way to gauge each candidate's comfort level interacting with the students in the building.

One important step to take at the beginning of the hiring process is to clarify for each participant what their role will be. Is this group tasked with identifying the single candidate to be recommended to the superintendent, or is this group advisory to the administration, tasked with prioritizing candidates and identifying the top two or three for further consideration? Whichever approach is taken, it should be made clear to the group from the outset in order to avoid hard feelings in the end if the top choice is overlooked.

2. See them teach.

The majority of hiring timelines provide opportunity for observing applicants in a setting analogous to that which they are seeking. If at all possible, school leaders should observe candidates prior to the final hiring being confirmed. In schools where this practice is employed, administrators indicate that the rank order of candidates has frequently changed after this step, when the highest-ranking candidate through the interview proved less than desirable when placed in front of children. There are several ways to do this, even with candidates who are working some distance away:

- Invite the candidate to teach in the school at which they are applying. This is the best way to determine their fit for the school, though the fact that they are working with students with whom they have no relationship must be considered. Limit observers in the room to one or two adults—typically those who students are accustomed to seeing—to provide the most authentic experience.

- Ask candidates to invite a member or two of the search team to their current classrooms, which will provide the best insight into how they build relationships with students and organize their instruction. This may be uncomfortable for the candidates and members of the visiting team as the host schools realize the purpose of the visit, making this a less-preferred approach, but a viable one nonetheless.
- Have the candidates set up a link so they may be observed in their current classrooms through a video platform. This is a good way to allow for the expectation that candidates will be seen teaching even if they are a long distance away or have difficulty scheduling live visits.
- Ask the candidate to record a lesson and share it with the team. This is the least effective way to get a sense of the teacher's effectiveness, due to the fact that the lesson can be selected from several the individual may choose to record. Still, this may be a viable option in the absence of other opportunities to see the candidate interact with students.

When observing candidates teaching in their own environment as opposed to the one to which they are applying, it is important that any observers understand what it is they are seeing and what it is they are looking for.

In one school where classroom observations of teaching candidates are common practice, the teachers on the visiting team were enamored with the candidate's intellectual interactions with his students. Unfortunately, they were observing a lesson at a selective private school, while the position being applied for was in a public high school, where not every student may come to school with the same advantages and motivations as those who are paying a steep annual tuition fee to attend. The instructor was hired and soon found that the position was not a good fit, either for him or the students, and a new hiring process was initiated the following year.

3. Obtain a writing sample.

One of the most visible and lasting ways educators present the school to the public is through their written communication. This includes, among other things, notes to students, emails to parents, and contributions to newsletters and websites. Misplaced apostrophes, overused commas, run-on sentences— all of these perpetuate common writing errors and present the school in an unflattering light to those who know better.

Asking each finalist to submit a timed writing sample can help identify candidates who may need assistance in this area or have significant challenges that may drop them lower on the recommended hiring list. Hiring teachers or school leaders with writing challenges creates more work for supervisors or others who must be assigned to proofread each communication of these individuals before it is sent, lest the school risk an error-filled letter being distributed or posted for many to observe.

4. Conduct a thorough background check.

It is surprising how frequently this step is missed when a school feels it has found the best candidate. Placing a call to the candidate's current or former employer is an absolute must, and asking the right questions is critical for preventing the hiring of individuals who may be, at best, poor instructors or, at worst, dangerous for kids. While many schools have a checklist of questions that may or may not flush out this information, one simple question school leaders may ask of previous employers is, "Is there any reason why this person would not be a viable candidate if you were hiring for the position they currently have in your school?"

Conducting an Internet search of the candidates is another easy way to see if there is confirming or concerning information in their past. This is particularly important in today's age of instant information, as every community has members who spend a good deal of time engaging in social media. Schools that do not conduct Internet searches of candidates in a structured way will find themselves at the center of a public firestorm if members of the community can quickly find information of a damaging nature to a candidate's reputation.

Internet searches should be overseen by the school's leadership and not discussed with selection committee members, as administrators must determine the level to which any concerns may rise. Legal counsel may need to be engaged before any final determinations are made regarding candidates for whom online content is troublesome.

5. Ask candidates how they will go beyond the classroom.

School climate and culture is set by those who work closely with students each day. At the middle and high school levels, in particular, students enjoy engaging in school-based activities that extend beyond the academic day. Whether it be in the arts, athletics, activities, or student government, these programs are best operated when the advisors or coaches understand how they align with the school's mission. Hiring educators who engage with students in sanctioned programming beyond the school day contributes to stronger relationships among students and teachers.

One question that should be asked during the interview is, "Are there clubs or activities you might be willing to advise or coach, and what experience do you have in any of these?" While the response should not be the defining reason why a candidate does or does not get offered the position, candidates who can easily identify appropriate ways in which they would like to work with students beyond the classroom may be more likely to develop trusting relationships with students and further the school's mission in an engaging way.

6. Provide candidates with the information they need to make an informed decision.

At the end of the hiring process, critical decisions must be made by the employer and the potential employee, and each of those decisions should be made based on accurate information. The school leader should begin building trust immediately by providing the candidate with information vital to their decision to accept the position (i.e., salary and benefits). A simple one- to two-page document with the pertinent information can be personalized for each new hire, further demonstrating the organization's professionalism and commitment to the candidate as an individual.

In short, schools should leave candidates with no surprises and no unanswered questions. Education is a profession, and educators should be treated as professionals. Providing the data necessary to make informed decisions is the first step the school leader can take to build a trusting relationship with new employees.

7. Make the difficult calls.

Most school leaders enjoy being the provider of good news. It is exciting to call prospective candidates to let them know they are being offered the position to which they applied. The energy and enthusiasm exhibited during these conversations reaffirm the hiring decision and typically leave both the caller and the recipient with a positive feeling.

On the other side of the coin are the calls that have to be made to those who interviewed but are not being offered the position. These calls must be made by the lead administrator overseeing the hiring process. Emails and voicemails do not cut it, nor does assigning this uncomfortable task to an administrative assistant.

Educators strive to be respected as professionals and therefore should be treated, and act, as such. As the leader of the organization, the administrator must develop the ability to deliver bad news. That news is often being communicated to a member of the community, someone who may be hired in a subsequent search, or possibly someone whose path will be crossed in a different setting years down the road. It behooves the leader to communicate with integrity and compassion directly to the unsuccessful candidates.

Leaving a message on voicemail or with a candidate's spouse or children (it has happened!), presents the administrator and the school in an unprofessional light and diminishes trust in the organization. Even to those applicants who may never interact with the school again, it is important that their experience with the school leader is one that is replete with trust. When school leaders take this small step to build trust with those with whom they interact only once, they are developing the skills necessary to build lasting trust with the constituents with whom they will work each day.

8. Create a hiring playbook.

The importance of the hiring process cannot be overstated, yet many schools leave this to chance. School leaders intent on hiring the best candidates should spell out the practices they will use in the process. A hiring playbook should be used to guide all school leaders through the hiring process, identifying the timeline, activities, and responsible parties at each step in the recruitment and hiring process, from creating and placing advertisements to the selection of final candidates.

Sample questions, interview activities, and training modules to help team members avoid asking illegal or biased questions are all important components of the hiring playbook. Leaders who invest the time in creating such a playbook will avoid confusion and increase the professionalism of the hiring process.

Onboarding and Retention

Once hired, educators are provided a great deal of autonomy. This is a necessary part of their development as instructors, given that they will be alone in the classroom with students for nearly the entirety of their careers. However, that autonomy should not come at the expense of quality instruction nor engagement in the school's overall mission. School leaders should take advantage of the opportunity to orient new hires as early as possible in their employment by committing funds to pay each new hire for several days of onboarding in a structured format.

The onboarding of new hires is a crucial step in promoting unity throughout the organization; not only does this introduce the school's mission, core values, and common practices to the new hires, it also helps to refocus those statements in the eyes of the school leaders.

Planning for a meaningful orientation process should be a significant focus for members of the leadership team each summer. Each member of the team, from the superintendent to grade-level leaders should participate in some way. A representative of the teachers' association should also be given the opportunity to present to the group. This is another way to foster trust with those who may be sitting across the table during negotiations or grievance hearings, and it only helps to develop a sense of collaboration in every possible setting.

Formal mentoring activities should continue through the first two years of their employment, with scheduled presentations to explain school policies and practices. It is important to cover topics that are important to the organization, but also include items that are of interest to the educators in the room. Showing concern for new staff as individuals is a meaningful way to build trust from their earliest days in the organization. Providing time for the group to raise questions of their own will help to shape topics for future years, as leaders become more aware of the types of concerns or curiosities expressed by the newest members of the staff.

In some cases, it may be advisable to wait a few months into the school year before identifying permanent mentors, allowing natural alliances to form between new hires and veteran staff members. Until those mentors are identified, team leaders within learning areas or grade levels may perform whatever mentoring duties are necessary.

As with the orientation sessions, the mentoring program may work best when there are formalized activities with appropriate compensation provided for the mentors. While classroom observations should be part of any mentoring program, those observations should not be part of the formal review process. It is best to keep the supportive nature of a mentoring relationship separate from any evaluative protocols, providing the new hire with the opportunity to take a few risks and try new practices without fear of reprisal.

From the moment a candidate interacts with the school at the start of the application process, through the interview, hiring, onboarding, and mentoring stages, the school leader has opportunities to build trust through clear communication, information sharing, orientation, and support. Treating each applicant, even those who are unsuccessful, with professionalism, dignity, and empathy is the mark of a competent leader.

With planning and collaboration, school leaders can and must take advantage of the opportunities provided when personnel openings occur. Defining the recruitment and hiring process, engaging others in the work, and ensuring protocols are in place to attract and retain candidates who will most benefit students are among the most impactful strategies leaders employ to build trust with students. In a school full of student-centered adults, the leader is afforded more opportunities to encourage innovation and empower others to take the lead in school improvement efforts. The real beneficiaries are the students.

Chapter 11

Rigidity, High Standards, and a Trusting Student Body

School leaders build trust with students by ensuring they are treated fairly while being held to high standards.

Just as the key to effective leadership of staff requires strong, trusting interpersonal relationships, the highest performing schools are led by administrators who encourage the staff to build similar relationships with students. From the time students step onto the school bus or arrive at school, every interaction they have with adults impacts the level of trust they have in the school.

It is clear that students learn best when they are in a safe environment—when they trust that their physical, emotional, and mental well-being are the priorities of the adults in the building. School leaders play a critical role in creating that environment, not only through setting clear expectations and modeling those expectations for the staff but also through their daily interactions with students.

In schools where trusting relationships are the norm among staff, a culture of collegiality and a sense of shared responsibility for continual improvement are fostered in all settings. In schools where this trust is extended to and experienced by students, there is an even higher engagement in academic and cocurricular programming, lower absenteeism and drop-outs, and stronger development of student voice and leadership skills. Students who feel seen feel safe; students who feel heard feel respected; students who enjoy positive relationships with teachers and peers want to come to school and are productive while they are there.

PROVIDING A SAFE SCHOOL WITH
REASONABLE EXPECTATIONS

Student trust in the school doesn't happen by accident—it is the result of intentional planning and implementation of structures and protocols that empower students to advocate safely for themselves and interact respectfully with the adults in the building. As was mentioned in chapter 10, this work begins by hiring and retaining student-centered educators who authentically care about the students with whom they are working.

If the school leader accomplishes little else over the course of a career, hiring the right people will make up for most other shortcomings. However, to go further, the leader must be willing to conduct an honest assessment of school practices, protocols, and policies, and address those that lead to diminished trust for students. This does not equate to a removal of standards and expectations; indeed, the application of a fair standard to all students is one of the best ways to build trust between the school and its constituents.

A common mistake made by school leaders is to assume that rules and regulations disempower students and lead to a breakdown in trust, but that is not the case. One must bear in mind that the vast majority of students appreciate the structure provided by reasonable policies, just as most citizens appreciate the structure provided by reasonable laws. The removal of such policies does not engender trust as some might assume, as many students rely on rules and protocols to provide them with safe, equitable opportunities to attend school.

Leaders who propose to remove expectations to demonstrate how much they trust the students are neglecting the fact that the rules they seek to abolish often provide the very structures that allow students to trust that the school cares about their well-being and development. For the majority of students, removing those structures leads to a loss of trust, rather than the opposite.

At the same time, leaders must be aware of unreasonable policies and practices that abound in some schools or classrooms. Some of these practices, implemented out of a stated desire to hold students to high standards, cross over the line of good reason and result in one quality that does not engender trust in any situation—rigidity. Addressing unreasonable practices of well-intentioned educators, some of whom may be a bit set in their ways, is a challenge for which the effective leader must be prepared.

Making the "high standards" argument is a fallback position educators often use when a decision they have made is being questioned. When this happens, school leaders are forced into that uncomfortable space between two approaches that should not be competing interests—backing the staff or applying reasonable standards for students. Unfortunately, in some situations, individual staff members may contribute to this conflict, mistaking rigidity for high standards. Helping them understand the difference can be a major challenge in interpersonal communication.

Clearly, teaching students how to follow directions and meet deadlines is an important role of the school. To not emphasize these points could lead to costly errors when the time comes to apply for jobs, purchase a home, or enroll in health insurance, but to be convinced that using the wrong color ink on a book report or handing in a science project five minutes late should discredit the entirety of the student's effort is nothing short of malpractice.

ENSURING A BALANCED APPROACH

To provide students the opportunity to attend a school with the desired blend of high expectations and tolerance for deviation, school leaders should conduct thorough reviews of school-wide and classroom-based practices. A few strategies that may be used to ensure a balanced approach are shared here:

1. Regularly review policy manuals and handbooks for reasonableness and consistency.

Often, complications of policies only become apparent when the time comes to enforce them. Take, for example, the high school in which the penalty for plagiarism is clearly spelled out as failure of the course. How plagiarism is defined or taught to the students is not specified, resulting in a very high bar being set for students with little support for helping them understand what is and is not plagiarism.

When a teacher arrives in the principal's office to report a situation in which a student quoted material from the Internet and neglected to cite the source, she feels justified in calling for the student to be denied credit for the course, as the policy indicates. But the matter can be complicated if the student is a senior who has been conditionally accepted at her college of choice and readily admits that she neglected to cite her source, claiming she did not realize she had to do so for such a short quote. Empathy may be the better course here, but a by-the-book teacher has the force of policy on her side.

School leaders would do well to spend time reviewing all policy manuals and handbooks and anticipating the scenarios that may lead to complicated implementation. Involving others in these reviews is critical. Staff members offer valuable insights into how various policies may impact students. Of course, at appropriate grade levels, student involvement in these discussions is empowering and necessary. Leaders should be prepared when students who engage in these processes often call for harsher standards than the adults who will have to impose them; tempering calls for policies with stiff penalties will be important.

Critical questions that should be asked about each policy include:

- Is this policy necessary, or would it be better to remove it and allow for administrative judgment?
- Do the penalties for violating the policy make sense to representatives from each constituent group?
- Will the administration be comfortable imposing the defined penalties?
- What are various scenarios that may make this policy difficult to enforce?

2. Avoid zero-tolerance policies.

Simply stated, zero-tolerance policies are rarely effective. Schools put them in place believing that a clearly stated, harsh penalty for noncompliance will ensure that no student ever breaks the rule. Were that the case, schools would create zero-tolerance policies for every situation and ensure a smooth-running operation each day of the year. Unfortunately, for every rule that is written, there is a student willing to break it, and schools must be prepared to enforce the penalties and/or restorative practices identified. Few things diminish trust in an organization faster than making exceptions for those that violate commonly agreed-upon standards.

3. Create restorative learning opportunities.

School leaders walk a fine line when it comes to student discipline. The call for stiff penalties as a deterrent for inappropriate behavior is one to which leaders may be drawn. Others may heed the call to understand the student's perspective and feel compelled to offer "another chance" to those who break the rules. Either approach employed exclusively will lead to a breakdown in trust that will cause long-term damage to the school. If schools are to truly be places of learning, leaders must avail themselves of opportunities to provide lessons when students make poor choices.

A restorative approach is often the more effective response, helping students to see how their actions harmed others and providing them the opportunity to repair the harm, rather than simply serving a sentence that has no educational value. Developing restorative consequences that educate as a first step will help reduce the need for harsher penalties for consistent offenders. Schools that focus on building trust *with* students must also build trust *among* students; the relationship-building, problem-solving approach of restorative practices is a necessary component of that effort.

4. Recognize that not every action sets precedent.

School leaders must be willing to make the tough call. There are moments when flexibility and compassion rule the day and moments when enforcement of prescribed penalties is well-advised. Leaders must avoid the temptation to create lengthy handbooks that cover every possibility, minimizing the need to make judgment calls. In reality, each situation will present its own set of circumstances, and the school leader should take the opportunity to hear each student's case. While a well-written rule serves as a guide to follow, a willingness to listen may result in changed behavior, which is one goal of meaningful education.

5. Act with consistency.

Once the policy manual and handbooks are updated, fair, and reasonable, the focus for the school leader turns to implementation. Accusations of favoritism spread rapidly in school communities; school leaders must be aware of that in every moment and provide a standard of consistency that builds confidence in their ability and willingness to treat each student fairly.

In many schools, a team of administrators works together to implement policy. It will be critical for those teams to communicate clearly how the standards will be applied. Whenever an exception is to be made by one member of the team, they should let others know what that exception is and why it is being considered. Making exceptions without communicating with team members creates a dichotomy of enforcement that harms the reputation of each member of the administration and leads to distrust by students.

Well-defined, collaboratively developed standards are a common characteristic of higher-performing schools. Consistent and equitable implementation is a foundational cornerstone in building trust between school leadership and students. With intentional focus given to enacting reasonable expectations with fair, learning-based consequences, school leaders foster trust not only with students but also with faculty and parents who may have increasingly divergent thoughts about student performance.

INTERACTING WITH STUDENTS
ON A PERSONAL LEVEL

A critical step in promoting positive interactions with students is being intentional about creating those interactions. For building principals, this starts with greeting students as they arrive at school each day. Meeting students in front of the school is an engaging way for school leaders to set the tone for the day. The added bonus at the elementary level is the trust that is built with parents who are delivering their children to school. Rather than being dropped at the curb and heading into a building with no sign of adults, children are being welcomed while the principal is waving to parents, letting them know, "we've got this; your child is safe."

Some superintendents make this an expectation of school principals at each level—up to and including the high school. For a truly student-centered school leader, there is no better way to start the day than by greeting the vast majority of students by name as they enter the school. For students who yearn for a safe place with caring adults, that initial contact can take a bit of the anxiety out of another challenging day at school.

The vibe continues as students enter the corridors and lobbies of the school. Adult presence is key, both at the start of the day and during passing times. Too often, teachers and administrators are distracted and remain in their classrooms and offices as students move throughout the building.

Imagine the difference in two scenarios for a student who is feeling bullied, anxious, or unsafe at school: In scenario A, the student walks through the corridors, surrounded by hundreds of classmates. There is no "safe" person in sight. It is a maze of youthful energy and intimidation—be that real or perceived. In scenario B, a teacher stands outside each classroom interacting with students, welcoming them to class, and engaging them in informal conversation. Their presence brings a sense of calm and safety to the youngster who deserves to feel safe at school.

Educators who balk at providing this level of supervision are forgetting what it is like to be a student, dismissing the angst that accompanies navigating the hallways and social structures of the school. Schools cannot just care about kids academically; they must also care about them social-emotionally. To separate the two is folly. Only when students feel safe are they able to focus academically and put forth their best effort to receive all that the school has to offer.

School-based leaders who are intentional about creating positive spaces to interact with students are among the highest performers in their field. One elementary principal built trust among students and staff by serving as a recess supervisor every day. This allowed one or two teachers each day to be relieved from recess duty, which is a gift that is never unappreciated. More importantly, the principal built relationships with students that will be remembered for a lifetime.

The principal didn't simply stand guard but participated as if recess were as much for the adults as for the students. From tossing a football to a group of fifth graders to pushing younger students on the swing, this school leader engaged students in a way that many adults never had. When the time came to ask those students to do something for the school, from keeping the cafeteria clean at lunchtime to putting forth their best effort on assessment exams, students responded with enthusiasm. They trusted their principal and knew that whatever was being asked of them was something they should approach with great effort.

In a similar way, one middle school principal made it part of his daily routine to eat lunch with a different set of students each day in the cafeteria. Again, the added bonus of providing teachers with administrative support during lunch duty is clear, but the relationship-building between school leader and students was even more impactful.

Rather than simply watching over the students as they ate, the principal would move from table to table throughout the month, enjoying the company of a different set of students each day. As lunch ended and students stepped outside for the remainder of the period, the principal would accompany them, often kicking a soccer ball with one group while talking with another about a book he had recently read.

With focused effort, this principal created a safe, trusting environment among staff and students, providing teachers with visible support as they performed one of the less popular duties of the day, interacting with students in a way that respected, yet modified, some of the norms of principal-student relationships.

Intentional action is required of school leaders with a vision of creating a school climate in which students are trusting participants. By providing students with safe environments where rules and expectations are reasonably developed and applied, school leaders can have a significant impact on school culture in a short period of time.

Part IV

TRUST BEYOND THE SCHOOLYARD

Chapter 12

Fostering Family Trust

These are their kids we're talking about.

Early in this text it was pointed out that the school leader is at the relational center of the school, though they should not position themselves as the focus of the school (see figure 1.1 in chapter 1 for a reminder). This concept is important to remember as school leaders move from discussing practical strategies for building trust *within* the school among staff and students to building trust *beyond* the school with families and community members.

While the vast majority of interactions, actions, and decisions that either foster or denigrate trust are those that directly impact staff and students, there is a different, but vital, aspect of the job in which the leader's relationships with families and the larger community may bolster confidence in the organization and allow for bolder steps to be taken toward the school's mission.

One of the greatest challenges in family relations is reconciling the different perspectives parents and educators bring to the table when discussing a student. While educators often claim, "I love my students," it must be recognized that, typically, there is no love like that which a parent has for their child. (The term "parent" is used throughout this text to refer to any individual who represents or has responsibility for caring for the child, although that person may be a stepparent, guardian, grandparent, or other legal or biological relation to the child.)

It is not uncommon to hear educators state their longing for "the good old days" when they believe families may have been more cooperative (or less disagreeable) regarding student-school interactions. In truth, it is likely that parent-school relations have been a mixed bag of support, collaboration, adversity, challenge, and congeniality since the dawn of public schooling, but the added components of social media and rapid communication have certainly intensified those relations in all ways—good and bad.

School leaders are provided daily opportunities to build trust with parents, sometimes through proactive communication and sometimes through crisis management. While consistent newsletters and announcements of upcoming events or student recognition are a staple of almost every school's communications plan, it is a school leader's willingness and ability to share less joyful news that will generate greater levels of trust among parents.

CONTROL THE NARRATIVE

With the proliferation of social media and smartphones in the hands of virtually every parent, staff member, and student of a certain age comes a greater likelihood that the school will not be the *first* provider of information about a school-based incident or event. However, thoughtful and timely notices can ensure that the school continues to be viewed as the most *accurate* source, and schools should make use of the technology at their disposal to keep parents informed as frequently as necessary about events taking place at the school. Planning for the unexpected, school leaders can take specific steps like those offered here to control the narrative about their school:

1. Create templates for a variety of communications.

Urgent situations (school evacuations, dismissals, etc.) require fast action by school leaders. While planning and practice are critical for proper handling of these events, nervousness and emotions can rise quickly when a real-life event occurs. Something as simple as a staff member smelling gas near the kitchen or a malfunctioning fire detection system can force evacuation of the school and raise anxiety among staff and students, many of whom will have their own mobile devices in hand, ready to broadcast to the world what they believe is happening. Within seconds of the evacuation being ordered, the news is out and parents are worried.

While the first priority for the school leader is to make sure everyone is safe, the next priority will be to communicate necessary information to staff and parents. Composing such a letter in the heat of the moment can be challenging. Having several templates stored in the school's communications system will be helpful. Creating the message for email, website, and social media formats allows the school to get official word out quickly. While these templates should be editable for the specific situation, thoughtfully crafting the message outside of the urgent situation leads to a lower likelihood of errors or emotional comments being made.

2. Don't be afraid to share the facts.

School leaders who do not shy away from sharing accurate information during an urgent situation will be more trusted by those with whom they are communicating. When leaders avoid sharing news, thinking it will reflect poorly on the school, they miss an opportunity to show the community that they can handle an intense situation, take care of the students and staff, and be open and forthright about the events of the day.

When communicating with parents during an urgent situation, school leaders should bear in mind that parents need to know several things:

- What is happening and how it is being addressed.
- That the students are safe.
- What is needed of parents—even if that is, "remain at work/home; your child is safe."

If the expectation is that students will be returning to class after an evacuation, the message should inform parents of that fact. When school leaders discourage parents from dismissing their children and spell out the schedule for the remainder of the day, the vast majority of parents will acquiesce. They want their children at school, and the school's communication will put them at ease and allow them to proceed with their day as scheduled. Leaving this piece of information out of any communication may lead parents to believe it might be a good idea to dismiss their child, which only adds to the confusion of the situation.

3. Reach out individually whenever possible.

Beyond the mass communications that occur proactively or in response to an urgent situation, school leaders have opportunities and a responsibility to build trust through individual communications with families. Sending a handwritten note or an email to a student's family to congratulate them on an accomplishment or placing a phone call to check in after an upsetting event are steps all school leaders should consider not just to build individual and organizational trust, but to authentically demonstrate concern for students.

4. Respond with a personal touch.

As with staff, many parents simply want to be heard. Whereas a phone call or visit to the school was the best way to do this prior to 2000, the twenty-first-century critic can sit at home and lodge complaints by email or social media. When dealing with an upset parent who has submitted a complaint by email, the best response proven over and over again is to pick up the phone and call them directly. In the majority of cases, a polite greeting from the school leader is disarming and leads to a positive discussion that provides an acceptable resolution. Whereas email is an exchange of *monologues*, a telephone conversation is a *dialogue*, with participants better able to understand one another's tone and intent.

If the immediate phone call is not an option, school leaders may want to consider a fairly standard email response that invites a conversation in the near future. Thanking the individual for sharing their thoughts and inviting them to speak at their earliest convenience is an approach that may help lower the temperature of the situation. This communication informs the parent that the school is taking the concern seriously while providing the school leader with an opportunity to do a bit of research with necessary staff members to gain greater insight into what the school's position might be.

5. Act with empathy.

The importance of the school leader's empathy for staff members was discussed in chapter 2, and its value should not be overlooked when considering communications with parents. While it may be tempting to be dismissive, the school leader must rise above and empathize with parents trying to protect someone who is most precious to them. Approaching each communication with that understanding firmly in place, the school leader is more capable of finding common ground in difficult situations.

Just as trust is built through personal relationships with staff and students within the school, so too must trust be fostered among those whose children attend the school. While many will appreciate more open communication of meaningful events and student accomplishments, some individuals will demand a more personal touch. School leaders must be prepared to pick up the phone or schedule in-person meetings in order to build relationships with supporters and critics alike.

When school leaders develop trusting relationships with parents, they solidify the third side of the education triangle (school—students—parents). Intentional effort to communicate openly and with empathy will affirm to parents that the school is, indeed, on the same team, with the best interests of students at the core of decision-making.

Chapter 13

Community Trust

In communities where trust is strong, resources will be provided with greater enthusiasm.

As aspiring school leaders progress through graduate school and certification programs, their focus remains largely on the internal structures of schools—those practices and policies that drive student and staff experiences each day. While work in this area attracts educators to leadership positions, it is important to note that they must also be prepared for another aspect of the job that has tremendous implications for how the school is viewed in the community: relating to the general public.

Through public presentations regarding items of importance (e.g., budget, curriculum, programming, policy), school leaders have multiple opportunities each year to interact with the public and build trusting relationships with the community. These are the taxpayers, alumni, family members, retirees, and residents who support the schools through a wide variety of activities. Without their engagement, the school will struggle to meet student needs as budgets will be challenged, volunteers will be hard to find, and new programs or policies will find little support where needed.

In communities where trust in the school is high, community engagement is viewed positively; schools are as well-funded as the capacity of the community allows, volunteerism in the schools is encouraged, and acknowledgement of the school's effectiveness is commonplace. In these communities, a noticeable number of alumni return to the community to avail their children of the same opportunities they experienced, and others move into town with the stated intent of taking advantage of the school's offerings.

At the same time, such communities have high expectations for their schools and school leaders. They have trusted, they have invested, they have engaged—and they expect results. They want to be assured that students are being provided their best opportunities for success, that programs are designed and implemented to promote development of critical skills and passions leading to prospects after graduation, and, most importantly for some, that schools are operating as efficiently as possible.

School leaders who understand the importance of community relations and take action to foster those relationships will enjoy a supportive and trusting environment that allows them and the instructional staff to avoid distractions that interfere with the core focus of the school.

When community trust is lacking or broken, students and staff suffer; volunteerism wanes, employment postings draw little interest, and opposition to the school program and budget can soon follow. While it may be typical for a sector of the community to support a more conservative approach to school finance, in a trusting community a strong contingent of supporters will band together to assist leadership in gaining approval of a reasonable proposal.

Not every decision school leaders make will be popular with all constituents. For some, the decision will impact them in a personal way, and they will react accordingly. It is critical that the leader understands the perspective of those who feel wronged. Responding in kind to angry citizens will only fracture the trust that can be fostered through conflicts and disagreements. Calm, composed responses will build trust—if not immediately with the detractor, at least with others who are observing the interaction.

RISING ABOVE

The thick skin necessary to absorb or deflect what appear to be personal attacks may not feel like a natural characteristic for many educators. Most teachers and school leaders enter and advance through the profession because they care about people and believe in the inherent goodness of people. When confronted with anger, it is difficult not to personalize the attacks. The ability to de-escalate, rather than intensify interactions, is a necessary skill for the trust-building leader. Several proven approaches for staying above the fray are worth consideration by leaders at all levels of the organization:

1. Don't make it personal.

Understanding human nature and the ease with which we have come to express displeasure with one another may help school leaders cope with public criticism. It is not personal for most critics, and when their concerns *are* personal, it is even more important that public leaders respond with understanding. Leaders must sift through the barbs and find the statements of truth that should be addressed in order to improve their own effectiveness, and that of the school.

2. Separate the idea from the personality.

Not every idea persistent school critics have may be a bad one. Demonstrating openness to those suggestions may crack the veneer of distrust some have developed. These individuals may have ten, twenty, or hundreds of ideas and criticisms that leaders are tempted to dismiss each year, but if they have any thoughts that should be considered, the leader must not let those opportunities go unheeded, especially if it benefits students. In these situations, it may be better to invite them in, talk to them about their idea, develop some common ground, and keep them apprised as the situation allows.

3. Give critics a voice and a seat at the table.

School leaders are called upon to calm turbulent waters that may be stirred up during challenging budget seasons or the implementation of new policies that challenge long-standing traditions. While it is more comforting to surround oneself with those of similar values and beliefs, it is important to extend an invitation to critics to participate in working groups where they may not share a popular viewpoint. Having their voices heard in earlier stages of planning may allow for development of a proposal that is more widely accepted by the community.

4. Get past the need to feel liked.

Yearning for the admiration of constituents can be problematic for those in leadership positions, as they must act with integrity and empathy as each situation demands, leaving the need for personal approval aside. The fact is, no matter how thoughtful or just a decision may be, nor how well it is communicated, there are going to be detractors and critics who will not approve. The leader who can set aside the need to feel liked, make decisions in the best interests of students, and share those decisions in clear, dignified communications will grow a deeper trust with the community than one who acquiesces in each moment to the sentiment in the room.

5. Learn from the criticisms.

Critics serve a useful purpose in the development of strong leaders. Imagine the young leader with no critics. Everything he or she does is met with praise or, at least, polite acceptance. There is no demand for growth or improvement, and the leader may become complacent. On the other hand, the leader who must prepare for criticism each week, whether at the faculty meeting, the school board meeting, or the leadership team meeting, is continually sharpening the tools necessary to quiet the critics and cast a wider net of collaboration.

This may be the greatest contribution of the leader's most vocal adversaries. Unbeknownst to them, they motivate the leader to prepare for interactions well ahead of time, gathering pertinent data, seeking a range of opinions, refining presentations, and crafting well-developed proposals that contemplate each perspective and possible outcome. Of course, it would be preferred that their protestations not be made in public, but one measure of the administrator's growth may be the decline in rancor exhibited over time by these vocal critics.

So long as the work being done is not simply to placate those who criticize, the leader can capitalize on the demanding nature of their opinions. Anticipating criticisms and questions, providing the data to support whatever recommendation is being made, and gathering input from a wide range of constituents, the leader can respond to harsh criticism with objectivity—calming those who come out in opposition and encouraging a healthy debate based on facts.

The majority of constituents will develop an acceptable level of trust when treated with dignity. How leaders respond to their most vocal critics will go a long way toward building trust among the larger community, as the majority of bystanders will form their conclusions about the leader's performance based on the interactions they observe the leader having with others. Being able to see through the personal nature of some attacks while seeking to understand the basis of the criticism is a skill all public leaders must develop.

COMMUNICATING WITH INTENTION

Developing community trust in the schools requires intentional action by school leaders to share accurate and timely information and to create an inviting environment in which community members engage with the school. The following suggestions have proven helpful in a variety of school settings:

1. Develop a communications plan.

Every school should have a robust communications platform, consisting of digital and/or hard copy newsletters, email distribution lists, social media and website postings, apps, and push notifications. Often, however, there is no clear understanding of which platform will be used for which types of communication, and by whom. When there is confusion within the organization as to who is communicating what to whom and by what method, there is assuredly confusion outside the organization as to how information will be received.

To ensure consistency of messaging, a plan should be developed and agreed upon by all who have the authority to distribute information through each system. Schools should prioritize communications by type and platform and create a matrix that clarifies how messages will be distributed. An excerpt of such a plan is illustrated in table 13.1. While an overview such as this is an efficient one-pager to clarify how each platform is to be used, a more detailed descriptor of the expectations within each platform is recommended prior to implementation.

Leaders should develop consistent formatting of postings and notices to provide a professional appearance for the school. One strategy for simplifying this approach is to set up templates that allow the user to simply enter the required information for each notice. It is recommended that the school's logo and motto be prominently displayed as a way to further the branding of the school. Consistency and branding not only provide a professional appearance but also limit the likelihood that messages sent by illegitimate accounts will be accepted as authentic—a concern of which school leaders must be keenly aware in the digital age.

Table 13.1   Communications Plan Overview

Type of Communication	Audience	Platform	Authorized User	Example
Emergency	Staff Families	Email Text Voicemail Social media Website	• Superintendent • Principal with superintendent's approval • Designee, with approval	• Evacuations, lockdowns
Urgent	Staff Families	Email Text Social media Website	• Superintendent • Principal	• School closure for inclement weather, items with limited time for response
Informational	Staff Families Community	Email Newsletter Social Media Website	• Superintendent • Principal • Others with approval of superintendent or principal	• Upcoming events, changes in scheduling, volunteer opportunities
Press Release	Community	News Outlets	• Superintendent • Principal with superintendent's approval	• Public meetings, special recognition

2. Limit broad communications to senior leadership.

While larger districts may have communications directors or PR personnel, the average-sized district will likely rely upon school- and district-level
administrators to oversee communication. In districts where others have the
ability to post to the website or distribute notices on a wide basis there is an
increased likelihood that a communication will be sent that becomes problematic for leadership.

Schools should limit the ability to send broad communications to those
in leadership positions (i.e., superintendent or principal), providing parents
and staff members a clear understanding of the source of the information.
Messages widely distributed from employees in other positions in the school
increase opportunities for mixed messaging and the appearance of disengaged
or disjointed leadership. Simply filtering these messages through the leadership ensures consistency of messaging, affirms the message has the support of
leadership, and signifies the importance of the message for all readers.

Parents want to hear from the principal and the superintendent; they want
to know their school leaders are engaged in every aspect of school life; they
want to trust that the leaders at the top of the organization are caring and
knowledgeable enough to address each topic of importance to their child's
education. Intentional dissemination of messages by leadership assists in
affirming that engagement.

3. Ensure access for all.

Recognizing the community as a critical partner, schools must ensure that
all constituents have access to information. With many community members
having limited exposure to the English language or the culture of American
education, schools must invest in systems that translate notices and information to a variety of languages and provide access according to the Americans
with Disabilities Act. Without specific effort to translate these notices, the
cultural divide widens and schools risk diminishing trust with those who are
most in need of an organization they can depend on.

4. Don't overdo it.

Attending conferences and professional development opportunities
throughout the country, school leaders have recently been encouraged to dive
into the world of social media by creating their own accounts and posting
snippets and tidbits about their day or blogging for the community. These
activities may have some merit but should certainly not be conducted at the
expense of the real work of leading the school. One danger of such activity is
oversaturation of information being distributed, which leads readers to begin
dismissing anything they receive, including urgent notices.

One first-year superintendent was excited to create his social media accounts and share images of his visits to classrooms and student activities each day. Unfortunately, he quickly became so prolific, teachers and parents began questioning how he had the time to be making social media posts several times each day. Within several months, senior leadership members became concerned that significant planning was being overlooked, details were being missed, and decisions were being rushed. Trust in the superintendent's ability to lead the schools evaporated, and by springtime the search for a new leader was initiated.

School leaders must avoid becoming so enamored with social media that it overtakes the important tasks that must be completed. The Greek poet Hesiod (700 BC) is credited with first saying, "moderation is best in all things." A posting every several days is more than enough to illustrate to followers how the school leader is engaged in the work of the students and staff, while signifying that there is plenty of important work to be done back at the office, as well. This also leaves capacity for recipients to fully read school messages, as they will be conditioned to understand that only meaningful information is distributed through direct communication.

5. Avoid jargon.

Communicating in ways the audience understands and relates to is a basic component of building trust. The use of jargon and "edu-speak" may disenfranchise an important sector of the community. When educators present information using acronyms and terms that are familiar only to those inside the school or those who have immersed themselves in the topic, they lose followers and diminish trust.

In every communication, prior to using acronyms, educators should spell out what it is that is being discussed. The job of the school leader is not just to inform, but to empower others to feel well-informed. Hiding behind jargon and acronyms diminishes that empowerment.

School leaders must operate with the confidence that what they are doing is just, and the more informed the public is, the more support will be generated for the schools. If this concept is ignored, leaders risk having only a handful of community members who are well-versed in matters of the district, and if that handful is of an opposing view, budget or project approval can become a very arduous process.

6. Share data proactively.

School leaders must present available data whenever possible whether that data supports their argument or presents a challenge that must be addressed. It is the sharing of the data itself that builds trust in the schools. When the data is positive, leaders should celebrate others who contributed to the success. When the data presents challenges, leaders must be prepared to adopt a collaboratively developed plan for improvement.

7. Respond to requests for information.

The Freedom of Information Act (FOIA) provides public access to a vast array of school documents. School leaders build trust among constituents when they increase the transparency with which the school operates. One way to do this is to respond courteously and quickly to FOIA requests. If the information being requested is, indeed, public information, then there should be no delay in responding in the affirmative and providing the documents identified.

School leaders who put up walls will break down trust. Citizens requesting information should not be presented with roadblocks; such a response will simply raise their suspicions further. If the school has nothing to hide, there's no need to act as if there is. If the school has reason to be embarrassed by public knowledge of a situation, the incident should not have occurred and the school leader must be prepared to address it. Either way, stonewalling members of the public when they make a request for information is an ill-advised approach. Being responsive and open with community members goes a long way toward de-escalating contentious requests.

Engaging parents and the community is an art that goes beyond making posts to social media platforms. Today's school leaders must find that balance between providing a safe, secure learning environment and welcoming the community into the school. Communication from all levels of the organization is the key to ensuring that community trust in the schools is well-placed, leading to appropriate levels of support being provided to carry out the mission.

Chapter 14

Meet the Press

The pen is mightier than the sword . . . and the internet beats them all.

"There's a reporter on the phone . . ." Six words that cause school leaders to reach for the antacids. What could they be calling about, now? Has a complaint been made about a teacher? Is there a disciplinary issue that hasn't been properly addressed? Does a staff member feel they've been mistreated? Any number of seemingly disastrous situations are envisioned. About the only thing that feels worse is when someone in the school says, "Did you know there's a camera crew setting up out front?"

School leaders must recognize the power of the press both as a vehicle for building public trust and as a force that can tear down any trust that previously existed. To capitalize on the press's potential for fostering trust in the school, leaders should take steps to build relationships with members of the press, collaborating to ensure stories are authentic and forthright and present information accurately. Leaving this to chance is a perilous approach to media relations.

When leaders and reporters are strangers to one another, there is a void that may be filled by assumptions of incompetence and poor intentions. Conversely, when media and school leaders are familiar with one another, they are more likely to trust one another and to treat each other fairly.

As with any other constituent with whom the school leader works, that trust is developed through frequent and meaningful interactions. With media personnel, those interactions may be less frequent, but they are certainly no less meaningful, as they are likely to be broadcast to thousands of others within moments, and the accuracy and fairness with which they are presented will go a long way toward determining the trust with which the leader is viewed.

BUILDING TRUST WHEN TIMES ARE GOOD

Just as schools are too often viewed by outsiders as purely bureaucratic institutions, so too is the media the victim of blanket statements and negative assumptions. Reporters are often stereotyped as sensationalists out to grab a headline or generate ratings. In reality the media is comprised of people with a wide range of ethical perspectives. The vast majority of them want to do a good job, reporting fairly and accurately the events of the day. Just as school leaders improve schools by building trust among constituents, they can improve media relations by building trust with individual reporters.

School leaders who foster trusting relationships with the media may soften the blows when controversial events or hard-hitting stories come their way—and those stories will come for every administrator who sticks around for more than a few years. Being proactive and deliberate about media relations is akin to putting money in the bank for a rainy day; school leaders should consider several approaches that will pay dividends in the long run:

1. Build relationships during noncontroversial times.

Fortunately, much of the school year passes without overt controversy, providing schools with a multitude of opportunities to share positive news with local media outlets. By providing stories and information on noncontroversial topics, school leaders make reporters' jobs easier and increase the likelihood that they will trust school leaders in more intense moments.

Proactive approaches to media relations go a long way toward mitigating the damage that could be done by a slanted news story on a controversial subject. Large school districts likely have a public relations (PR) department, while smaller districts are left scrambling whenever the media calls, but even in districts with limited resources a system for informing the media of good things happening in the district may be developed.

One small district tried the approach of providing a PR stipend to a part-time employee, encouraging principals and other school leaders to notify the individual of special events at their schools. The employee would attend each event, snap several pictures, jot down a few quotes, and write up a short press release to be posted to the school's website and released to the media. While many of the stories were not published by the media, the conduit had been created and the media was more in tune with what was happening in the schools on a daily basis—and therefore less likely to adopt an oppositional stance quickly.

Other districts have done this through the use of volunteers from organizations such as parent-teacher groups or educational foundations. The benefit of this approach is that trust is also being fostered with those groups, as their contributions are being valued by the school leadership.

2. Be responsive.

Responding to requests for information is one of the easiest and most consistent ways to build trust with the media. Media outlets need information, and they thrive on primary sources. Leaders who provide a quote or two for school-related stories each time a request is made find that cooperation pays off when reporters call regarding stories that are less comfortable.

On the flip side, one of the most damning statements made at the end of news reports is, "The school administration did not respond to our request for a comment on this story." To be fair, this is not always an accurate representation of fact, but it is close enough to be justified by the news organization.

As an example, one school leader was justifiably upset to have read in Sunday's newspaper that the school had not returned the reporter's call for a comment. The leader arrived at school on Monday morning to find a voice-mail left by a reporter in the main office in-box Saturday evening, which led to the unfair representation of facts in the article.

To avoid situations like this, leaders should make sure local news outlets have an email address that is checked consistently, even on weekends and nonschool days. The extra effort to provide a statement on a Sunday afternoon will be worth it on Monday morning, as the "no comment" statement brings about more suspicion by those reading or viewing the story, breaking down the trust between the public and the school.

3. Prepare for each interaction.

Although many school leaders feel confident handling a wide range of controversies on the fly, meeting with the media requires a different approach. Reporters are not going to include lengthy, time-consuming explanations on air or in print. They require short, concise statements that address the heart of the matter in order to craft their story to meet their producer's demands. Because of those parameters, communicating with the press is unlike communicating with any other entity or individual; it requires thought and intentionality of a different nature.

One approach is to ask reporters of print media to send their questions via email and indicate their deadline for writing the story. This shows respect for their work and provides the school leader the opportunity to craft responses that make sense and are properly worded.

Quoting someone accurately is a challenging task for some reporters, and school leaders cannot afford to be misquoted or misinterpreted. Submitting written responses ensures greater accuracy and makes the reporter's job easier, as statements are already typed up and confirmed as accurate. Meeting the reporter's deadline with plenty of time to spare and providing several meaningful quotes will build confidence in the administrator and promote a trusting relationship.

Similarly, on-camera interviews require preparation and focus. Before engaging in live or taped interviews, school leaders should identify two or three key statements and one underlying theme that can be reiterated in several ways. It is important to remember that the aired interview will likely include, at most, two or three clips of ten-second quotes. A coherent but lengthy statement will end up on the cutting room floor.

The public watching the story wants to see a school leader who is articulate and prepared. Stumbling through an interview will diminish the trust the public has in the individual and the organization. Providing several crisp, coherent statements will give them confidence that the leader is addressing any concerns appropriately.

This approach is demonstrated over and over again in two of the most televised activities of this generation: sports and politics. Watching large market celebrities, professional sports coaches and high-level politicians engage with the media provides lessons every school leader should heed:

• Know the material before going on camera,
• Stick to the organization's message and position,
• Avoid demonstrating frustration or anger, and
• Tell the truth without violating confidentiality.

The majority of controversial subjects that result in media attention are related in some way to student safety. Clearly, every school leader identifies students' emotional and physical well-being as one of their core responsibilities—and one they accept with a great deal of passion. Still, there will be accusations and incidents of bullying and harassment that make their way into the media.

Rather than assuming a defensive posture when these allegations are made, the school leader should be prepared to stand before the cameras and affirm that student safety is their number one concern, that their policies prohibit such behaviors, that all allegations are immediately and fully investigated, and that the district will continue to provide students and staff with the training necessary to eliminate these incidents from the school. Avoiding the specifics of any individual allegations is important, but reassuring the public that the school does not dismiss such allegations out of hand is also critical.

Intentionally preparing for the interaction with the media provides the school leader a decent shot at improving trust with the public, rather than allowing deterioration that may occur from a damaging story.

4. Follow-up after the story is released.

Reaching out to a reporter or editor following a story is not a common practice, but it is one that engenders positive relationships. When a reporter provides an accurate representation of the facts, treats the school and the leader fairly, or promotes a school event or accomplishment, a quick note to the reporter to thank them for their work is an effective way to further the collegiality that can develop between the media and the school.

In similar fashion, speaking with the news organization if the school was mistreated may help set clear parameters for the relationship moving forward. The school leader who was accused of not responding to the media's inquiry contacted the reporter and editor the following day to express her displeasure with the mischaracterization and received an apology (though not a retraction) from both. More importantly, the outlet was provided feedback that inaccurate representations were not acceptable. Confronting poor behavior respectfully and with conviction is one more way to build trust with constituents on all fronts.

Just like educators, journalists need to earn a living, and they approach their duties with moral conviction. Still, in order to get paid, they need to sell subscriptions and advertisements, and to do so they must produce stories that catch the reader's attention, especially those that contain controversy, conspiracy, or salacious content. Any indication that the public has misplaced its trust in the school is going to check all the boxes for a newsworthy story and potentially earn the reporter the above-the-fold headline that will hang in their office for years to come.

Proactive relationship-building with media personnel can prevent, or at the very least, minimize, reputational damage that results when a controversial matter becomes public. Laying a foundation of trust through interpersonal communication and a willingness to engage will improve the likelihood of favorable coverage when things go awry.

Part V

TRUST AT THE LEADERSHIP LEVEL

Chapter 15

Leading the Board

The School Board's role is not to manage the school, but to ensure that the schools are well-managed.

While the trusting relationships developed between the school leader and constituent groups within the school—students and staff—are the most important for moving the school forward on a day-to-day basis, it is often the relationships with groups outside the school—the parents and community members—that have the most significant impact on the perceived effectiveness and length of the leader's tenure. Clearly, the school board comprises a critical group in this constituency.

While a few upset students, staff members, or parents can certainly make for a difficult day and are not to be dismissed, a few upset school board members can disrupt an entire career. When the working relationship between the school leader and the board is based on trust, a model is set for the rest of the district, providing a level of confidence throughout the community that promotes stability, progress, and collaboration.

While most board members run for office for altruistic reasons, every school leader will experience challenging members at some point. The most demanding board members serve a very useful purpose, motivating school leaders to prepare to the extreme. While agreeable, flexible board members may be more enjoyable to interact with, it is often the more critical members who help school leaders improve their craft. These members do not allow for sloppy presentations of disjointed or irrelevant data; they expect clarity of purpose and a clear explanation of the costs and benefits of proposals.

Such individuals do not buy educational jargon and they question conventional ideas. In short, they encourage leaders to perform at a higher level, preparing the school leader for the questions and criticisms that may come from a less trusting sector of the population, providing insight into the thinking of the most vocal opponents of the school's mission and performance.

Rather than dismissing the harshest school critics as a meddlesome minority, nurturing a meaningful, respectful relationship with board members provides the leader with a stronger base and a greater likelihood of success when troubles arise in the future.

DEFINING THE ROLE OF THE BOARD

School leaders must be intentional about their work with the school board. From the moment an individual is elected (and, likely, before), a relationship is being formed with the school leader. The individual relationships between school leader and board members are critical to the school's culture, climate, and long-term performance. There are many strategies to consider that strengthen those relationships and provide the board with a sense of purpose, including:

1. Develop a board handbook.

Board members want to know the parameters of their work, and school leaders have a responsibility to guide their understanding. Many districts produce a board handbook, which includes the most relevant board policies—those regarding board meetings, conflicts of interest, operational procedures, freedom of information training, and legislation or protocols important to the board's work. This handbook should be updated and provided to each member annually.

2. Provide annual training.

Whether through the hiring of a consultant, the board's attorney, or a state agency, providing professional development for the board at the outset of each year is an impactful way to help members understand their role. A day-long retreat provides an opportunity to set a professional and collegial tone for the year.

The school leader should work with the board chair and the training facilitator to set the agenda and highlight important points to be emphasized in the training, based on the board's makeup. One approach that has proven to be effective is to focus the first half of the day on board operating procedures to lay the foundation for how the board will function throughout the year. The afternoon can be spent reviewing the district's strategic plan and other timely items to identify a set of annual goals for the board and the superintendent.

3. Build coalitions where possible.

Even with the most oppositional board member, a superintendent will likely find instances where agreement is shared. In those instances, it is important to affirm that solidarity, so as to convey a sense of fairness and objectivity. The most effective school leaders are able to find rays of hope in every relationship and convey to those individuals their opinion is valued and they will be treated with dignity. By highlighting areas of commonality, the school leader provides opportunities for these individuals to feel respected and better able to work with others.

4. Encourage communication with board leadership.

The relationship between the administrator and board leadership is critical for efficient operations at the board level. While keeping the entire board apprised of situations that may cause concern or rumors to spread throughout the community, it is especially important for the superintendent to be in close contact with board leadership. Most importantly, the superintendent should ensure that board members understand that they may hear about events or situations at school at the same time as many members of the community.

The expectation that board members will be told everything that happens in the schools before anyone else must be dispelled at the start of each year. Still, providing members with additional information whenever possible is typically a good idea, giving them confidence that they have the knowledge necessary to assist the administration in pushing out only accurate and helpful information.

Strategies for ensuring effective communication between leadership and the board include:

a. Plan and prepare each agenda collaboratively.

Weekly discussions should be held between school leadership and board leadership to address meeting agendas, workshop topics, and any current or anticipated situations. The board leadership should keep the superintendent apprised of concerns or questions they are hearing from constituents or other board members. Scheduling a weekly appointment to discuss the agenda for any upcoming meetings is one good way to do this while also providing some parameters by which the board leadership abides.

Running through the upcoming agenda, identifying potential sticking points and the likely questions to be asked provides both the board leader and the superintendent with an opportunity to anticipate how best to present items and manage any controversial topics.

b. Provide as-needed notifications.

If boundaries are not an issue for the board chair, the superintendent may choose a more fluid arrangement in which communication occurs purely as deemed necessary. While the agenda meeting should be a standing appointment, communicating items of importance to board leadership is a critical way to build trust.

5. Provide extensive backup well ahead of meetings.

One of the best ways to build trust with members of the board is to ensure they have all the information necessary to consider administrative proposals well ahead of each meeting. Approximately one week prior to the meeting, board members should be provided with a copy of the agenda and any backup materials necessary to fully explain each item.

An efficient way to do this is for the superintendent to present introductory remarks for each item on the agenda. For example, a new policy on concussion management may be introduced by a short paragraph indicating that this policy is required by law and addresses the need for medical engagement in order for students to return to school or activities. The descriptor may provide information about the origin of the policy, who was involved in writing it, whether it has been vetted by attorneys, and any relevant data that may be of interest to the board.

This sort of backup takes significant effort and organization each week, but the pay-off is a smooth, efficient board meeting. Answering questions before they are asked, this approach simply shifts the time spent explaining a topic from the meeting to the days prior to the meeting. Board members attend the meeting well-informed, asking their questions with more confidence and focused on the topic at hand. Going a step further, the superintendent may also provide any suggested motions, which could remove some of the awkwardness some members feel when attempting to formalize a motion.

Any presentations that will be made during the meeting should be included with the backup. This may put added pressure on school leaders who struggle to manage their time well. The downside of not doing this is that the board will not have the opportunity to notify the superintendent of potential questions ahead of the meeting, making for a less predictable outcome. The upside is an appreciative board participating in a more informed manner.

6. Script meetings for new leadership.

Most superintendents will work with several new board leaders during their tenure. Often, these individuals are new to leadership, or may not be well-versed in the protocols adopted for meeting operations (parliamentary procedure, Robert's Rules, etc.). While agenda meetings with the board chair are helpful for leadership to understand what will be presented, a script of the meeting, at least in the first few months of the year, will help the new chair develop rhythms necessary to facilitate the meeting efficiently.

Clearly, the meeting cannot be scripted in terms of what others may say, but typing up the call to order, the introduction of items, and the proposed motions on each item will provide the chairperson with language that will make board members more comfortable. Within a few months, this script will no longer be needed, but providing it early in the year gives the chairperson confidence and comfort in the knowledge that the superintendent has their back. Building a sense of teamwork and supportive collaboration with the chair goes a long way toward building trust with the entire board.

7. Agree to "no surprises"—from either direction.

Every superintendent has experienced the sinking feeling that comes when a board member raises unforeseen concerns or questions that derail a public meeting. The same is true for board members who arrive at a meeting to find a new item on the agenda for which they had no forewarning. No one appreciates being surprised in a public meeting by proposals they were not expecting.

To avoid this, school leaders should come to agreement with the board at the start of each year that all will do their best not to surprise one another during public meetings. The superintendent can meet this standard by sharing proposals and relevant data well in advance of each meeting. Board members can do this by letting the superintendent know of their concerns and questions, to a large extent, in advance of the meeting.

This is not intended to stifle conversation or stage the meeting, but purely to give each participant a heads-up as to the perspectives that may be shared and the data that may be presented or sought prior to gathering in public. When Boards operate with this basic tenet, meetings are productive and efficient and the participants trust one another to be forthright and transparent, allowing for greater functionality.

The superintendent's role in this process is to submit the agenda and any backup materials to the members approximately one week ahead of any meeting. This provides the members the opportunity to read through the material and inform the superintendent of any additional pieces of information they may seek. It should not be expected that members will avoid asking other questions at the meeting, but if they are conditioned to let the superintendent know of the types of information they may be seeking ahead of time, it will also make any follow-up questions easier to answer when the time comes.

8. Conduct program review prior to major shifts.

Clearly, budget development is one of the most arduous tasks for the school leader and the board each year. Adhering to the "no surprises" rule, big-ticket items that will be proposed in the budget should also be introduced to the board well ahead of the budget proposal. One way to do this is by conducting "program reviews" throughout the year, targeting specific programs which the school leadership or board identify as addressing areas of need. For example, a district seeking to add pre-kindergarten programming should present a well-researched proposal to help the board understand the needs and costs well in advance.

During program review, the appropriate staff provide data, information, and recommendations to the board as part of a public presentation, allowing members to share their own questions and observations. The board's input is helpful for the administration to understand what support there may be for the proposed changes, and the plan is refined prior to budget season.

9. Create and maintain a blueprint for the year.

The board should have a clear vision for its work from the outset of the school year. One tangible way to do this is to create a blueprint identifying each meeting of the full board and any subcommittees, identifying as much as possible the agenda and program review items that will be addressed at each. This gives the board and the public an overview of the areas of focus for the year, while also providing the administration with a clear understanding of the items to be presented at each meeting. A simple format for this blueprint is provided in table 15.1.

Following the blueprint as closely as possible while remaining flexible in the face of unforeseen events allows the board and administration to work collaboratively with an understanding of where they are headed and how each participant contributes to the progress. Publishing the blueprint and keeping it updated as changes are made builds trust throughout the community that school leadership has a steady hand at the helm and a clear vision for the work of the district.

Table 15.1   Sample Annual Blueprint

Meeting	Day/Date	Time	Location	Agenda Items
School Board Business Meeting	Monday, 9/13	7:00 p.m.	Board Room	• Opening of School reports • Enrollment data review
Finance Committee	Tuesday, 9/21	8:30 a.m.	Conference Room	• Key metrics • Audit
School Board Workshop	Monday, 9/27	7:00 p.m.	Board Room	• Program Review: Outsourcing Transportation

10. Keep policies handy during meetings.

One of the more practical things the school leader can do to support the board is to ensure that the board is following its own policies. Having a notebook (digital or hard copy) at each meeting, with key policies handy, helps the board avoid embarrassing missteps when meetings become contentious.

Many boards claim to follow a specific set of protocols for their meetings. Parliamentarians may be able to cite when certain motions require a two-third majority or an end to any debate, but most board members are not going to recite the many rules that accompany such procedures. Preparing a simple guide that explains each type of motion and how it is administered will save the board from procedural missteps that may come back to bite them later.

Board meeting policies should be kept handy for those moments when heated public debate or lengthy meetings become a concern. Local policy will determine how members of the public may participate in the meeting, and at what time all business shall cease.

11. Avoid the rubber stamp label.

While efficiency in board meetings is appreciated, it is important that boards find that sweet spot that exists somewhere between the two extremes of trusting the administration complicity and questioning every move. Healthy deliberations should be encouraged while repetitious conversation is to be avoided.

One concern expressed by board members in districts where efficiency is emphasized is that they are viewed as rubber stampers of the superintendent's leadership. On the other hand, in districts where lengthy board meetings are the norm, the superintendent feels mistrusted and the community feels the board cannot make a decision. Neither arrangement is productive for the long-term health of the district.

To help the board feel engaged and validated while avoiding laborious discussions, the chair must become adept at facilitating debate effectively by following a few simple protocols:

- Stick to the motion on the table; do not allow comments to steer the discussion away from the topic at hand.
- Allow each person to speak once before anyone speaks twice; this promotes conciseness and allows quieter members the opportunity to share their thoughts.
- Expect that all questions go through the chair to limit back and forth debate among members and between members and the administration/public.
- End the debate when statements become repetitious. After each member has shared their perspective and heard from others, the board chair should

move toward a vote before comments simply become restatements of prior discussion.

- Accept that not every vote will be unanimous. While it is important to have unity on many issues, there may be moments when some members will vote in opposition to a motion, which is entirely acceptable if they are to be allowed to vote their conscience.

12. Minimize the number of subcommittees.

Where there is mistrust in any organization, there will most likely be a committee set up to fix the problem. Countless examples abound, and school leaders are encouraged to examine the committees in their districts to determine why they exist and if they are necessary or helpful.

The school board's responsibilities lie in several main areas:

- Employment of the superintendent
- Setting of policy and curriculum
- Adoption of a school budget

Almost everything for which a school board is responsible falls under these headings. Because the entire board will be engaged in supervising the superintendent, there are only two subcommittees of the school board necessary for proper oversight of the schools:

- Finance
- Policy

It is not uncommon to find board involvement in a range of other areas, resulting in the formation of various standing committees such as Personnel, Communications, Curriculum, and other subjects that fall within the superintendent's realm of responsibility. In an efficient district, these areas are managed internally by school leadership, while the board's oversight of the superintendent provides the checks and balances necessary to promote the performance expected in all areas.

Typically, standing committees are formed because of an event that disrupted operations and led members of the board to determine that school personnel were no longer capable of overseeing these areas. School leaders who engender trust with the board minimize the expansion of subcommittee work at the board level, possibly even disbanding existing committees whose work is better done by the educators in the district and reported to the full board as necessary for adoption.

This is not to say that committees should not be formed for time-sensitive work that requires greater input from the board and community, such as when a strategic plan is being developed or a major construction project is in the works. Forming working groups to engage a broader range of constituents in matters of significance is a necessary step in building trust with the broader community.

13. Be the filter.

The superintendent is in a unique position, situated directly between the board and all employees in the district. While all should be working toward the same outcomes, there will be moments when the groups disagree on how to reach those outcomes. The school leader must be the filter between all groups, serving as peacemaker, lead negotiator, and compromiser.

When a board member makes a statement that may be incendiary toward teachers, when staff members complain that the school board is out of touch, or when negotiations with one of the labor unions become confrontational, the administrator has a responsibility to quiet the storm rather than fuel the fire. Filtering out the noise and negativity, the school leader helps each group hear the perspective of others without the emotion, but with all of the necessary information to bring about peaceful resolutions and progress.

A school leader's greatest likelihood of a short tenure lies in a broken relationship with the school board. A trusting relationship at this level of the organization is necessary for efficient and effective management of the school; responsibility for fostering this relationship lies squarely on the leader.

Chapter 16

A Mission of Trust

Good schools provide students with meaningful, well-administered opportunities in a variety of disciplines. Great schools do it in a coordinated, collaborative fashion in which everyone understands the mission and their role in advancing it.

Driving through an unfamiliar part of the country today is certainly not the disconcerting challenge that it was just a few short years ago. Navigation systems programmed directly into mobile devices and automobiles have relieved the stress and anxiety of determining how best to get from one location to another. The technology even suggests the fastest route to get there, taking into consideration road construction, speed limits, and up-to-the-minute traffic conditions.

While these high-tech navigation systems receive a tremendous amount of data from various sources in order to guide the driver along a preferred route, nothing can happen without the driver first inputting the most critical piece of information—the desired destination. Without that identified end point, the system may lead the driver on an enjoyable ride, with smooth roads and stunning scenery, but arrival at the preferred address will be a hit or miss proposition. With the destination clearly stated and accurately entered, the passengers trust they are headed in the right direction, aided by external markers reassuring them of the accuracy of their chosen route.

The analogy to schools is clear: leaders and constituents must have a clear understanding of where the school is headed, and what it will stand for along the way, if the school is to create the best opportunities for moving effectively toward its destination.

While it might be safely assumed that the vast majority of educators working in a school share similar values and views about their role at the school and the school's role in the community, the lack of a common set of core beliefs and a consistently applied mission statement can result in organizational mistrust and disenfranchised constituents. Conversely, schools with clearly defined, collaboratively developed, and consistently applied mission statements provide a framework of trust to which staff, students, and other constituents may cling when engaging with the organization in any number of settings.

MISSION MATTERS

When asked to seek out their school's mission statement and describe how it drives decision-making at their school, graduate students aspiring to become school leaders report a wide range of findings. Typically, a significant cohort report having no knowledge of the school's mission and struggling to find anyone who does. Others suspect they can find the mission "somewhere on the school's webpage" but have little experience focusing on it during their day-to-day work at the school.

The very few fortunate enough to be working at higher-performing schools do not need to look up their district's mission—they know it by heart, typically because it is a clear, concise statement that is highly visible throughout the school and frequently referenced in their daily interactions.

When these same graduate students are asked to speak with *students* about the school's mission and their familiarity with it, the results weaken considerably. Although they may attend school where the mission is widely distributed, the degree to which it is used to drive decision-making in the school varies within a much narrower continuum, with most answers falling between "never" and "occasionally."

Whether they can easily point to examples of putting their mission into practice, most educators work in schools where the vast majority of staff members are doing the best they can to provide quality opportunities for students. Many speak articulately about their own view of what the school's mission should be, and those views, at their core, may be fairly consistent with others in their setting. However, without a collaboratively developed and frequently referenced mission for the school, individual interpretations can lead to disjointed programming, retracting of efforts, and confusion that erodes trust in the organization.

The fact that many schools are doing good work for students without a widely known and adhered-to mission statement is likely a result of the fact that most educators have developed for themselves an interpretation of educational mission that is fairly consistent with that of their colleagues.

As a result, for decades public schools simply pushed forward with the day-to-day tasks of educating students. Over time, though, schooling has become more and more complex as schools have become the provider of services far beyond the scope originally envisioned by the earliest school leaders.

From the one-room schoolhouse with a single teacher for all grades to vast organizations that include library-media specialists, technology integrators, and life skills teachers, along with social workers, counselors, nurses, and police officers, the responsibilities of America's schools have grown exponentially, demanding that each school clearly articulate the organization's mission and goals.

While it is recognized that schools differ from for-profit corporations, it does not preclude school leaders from learning from their counterparts in the corporate sector. The adoption and implementation of mission statements is one significant area where this is most applicable. Successful (i.e., trust-filled) organizations in the private sector tend to have simple, clearly stated, and easily adopted mission statements that are shared at all levels of the organization, from the executive suite to the warehouse and everywhere in between.

Just as for-profit organizations understand the need to adopt, promote, and strive to embody simply stated missions, so too must America's schools. Organizations lacking a mission lack direction. In schools without a clear mission, the intuitive nature of educators may provide students with learning opportunities, there is no doubt. But, like the family that follows their car's navigational system without first selecting their destination, the school will meander its way along an undetermined path, with no clear understanding of where it is headed.

Only slightly better than having no mission statement at all are the schools that create lengthy, complicated mission statements in an apparent attempt to address every situation that may arise in the course of a year. These statements, though well-meant in their creation, simply lead to confusion, frustration, and eventually dismissal. Nobody can recall what they say, and few can accurately interpret what they mean.

The school's mission can and should be stated quite simply. A concise, focused mission leads to more likely buy-in from all constituents; it is accessible for staff, students, and community members and transferable to the daily work of the district.

In schools where the mission is pervasive, it drives the direction of the school and helps clarify policy and practice. To guide the school to that place, leaders must understand the need for a universally adopted mission. Once that understanding is gained, facilitation of mission development and implementation begins.

DEVELOPMENT AND IMPLEMENTATION
OF MISSION STATEMENTS

Mission development may seem a daunting task for school leaders, with so much else to dominate their daily schedule. However, committing to this work and laying out a plan for completion will keep the organization on course. What follows is not a prescriptive format for developing a mission statement, but suggested strategies that have proven successful in mission-driven, high-performing schools:

1. Collaboratively develop the mission statement.

Schools that already have a mission statement may determine it is time to conduct a review of existing documents as they begin the process of refocusing the school. There may not be a need to dismiss what has been documented previously. In fact, there is something to be said for honoring the work of predecessors, some of whom are likely still in the district. It is also important to recognize that the mission of the school may not be any different than it was when a previous statement was developed—and change for change's sake should be avoided—but it may be that the existing mission can be stated more succinctly.

To guide the school through development or review of its mission, school leaders should consider several approaches:

• Give serious consideration to leading this work in a hands-on manner.

While many consultants are eager to facilitate this work, the school leader should not dismiss this opportunity to lead. Serving as the voice of the school while developing or refining the mission statement demonstrates buy-in of the leader indicates the priority this work has been given and sets the tone for collaboration and mission-driven work going forward.

The school leader who guides the school community in this task, providing a forum for all to be heard, will build collateral with constituents throughout the district and lay the foundation for trusting relationships. Consultants may still be used in the background to coach leadership teams through the process but having the leader of the organization out front in this effort is meaningful.

• Invite representatives from throughout the district.

Including staff from each of the schools (parents, community leaders, and students) to serve on the mission review committee allows for a variety of perspectives. This will be helpful and lead to greater buy-in throughout the community.

• Have the school board develop and formally adopt a charge for the committee, with a well-defined timeline limiting the length and frequency of meetings, authority and duration of the committee, and reporting mechanisms.

This highlights the importance of the work and indicates the school board's desire to engage the staff and community in its efforts. The committee should be advisory to the school leadership, be that the administration or the school board, with final authority for adoption resting with the proper governing body for the school or district.

• Develop and stick to a well-defined time frame.

Twelve months should be short enough to allow for sustained effort and long enough to complete this work. Meeting length should be limited to ninety minutes or less to keep the group fresh and energized.

• Provide historical documents regarding existing or previous mission statements.

It is vital to honor the work of previous committees and consider all available data before making significant changes to existing statements.

• Share brief articles that explain the importance of mission statements and their application in high-performing organizations.

An informed committee will be more likely to adopt a mission statement and core values in the students' and school's best interests.

• Review sample mission statements from highly regarded schools or organizations.

There is no need to reinvent the wheel; with hundreds of districts doing this work each year, a wealth of information is readily available to anyone willing to look for it. By shining a spotlight on models that are concise, focused, and easily remembered, school leaders encourage quality work by their own team.

• Gather input from school staff and community members, both electronically and in-person.

A simple survey can provide a great deal of data that may reinforce an existing mission statement or indicate need for a shift. Staff meetings and public forums, held once at the beginning of the process for initial input and once near the end of the process to review the proposed mission statement,

promote the importance of this work and provide for greater buy-in throughout the school and community.

- Adopt a shorter version of the mission statement that could be used as the
  district's motto.

This provides another way to make the mission accessible to a wider audience. While the mission statement itself may require a bit more text, a concise
slogan can capture the essence of the mission and be used to brand the school
in a meaningful way.

2. Intentionally promote the mission as a centerpiece of the school's work.

Promotion of the school's mission is not a *sometime* thing—it is an *all-the-
time* thing, starting from the moment a teacher is hired, a student enrolls in the
district, or a family moves to the community. Countless opportunities exist
for declaring what the school is about. While some approaches are superficial,
when combined with more substantive strategies they create a school culture
where everyone is aware of the core beliefs that drive the work.

- Highlight the mission during orientation programs for new staff.

While the sessions may be led by various school administrators, the organizational leader should consider speaking to new staff about the school's
mission. This is a powerful opportunity to show the extent to which the mission is embraced at the leadership level and the level to which it is expected
to influence the work of everyone in the school.

- Reinforce the mission in highly visible settings at the start of each school
  year.

The annual reopening of schools provides an opportunity for the leader to
present the mission statement and core beliefs in a new light. While each year
brings its own challenges and areas of particular concern, the central mission
of the school remains firm and should provide a foundation from which to
address those changing demands. District leaders must seize this chance to
renew their commitment to the mission and present examples of how the
district's work will align with the mission in the coming year.

School-level leaders have a similar opportunity with staff at the start of
the school year, and even greater opportunities during assemblies and open
houses to reach students and parents with this messaging. Without school-
wide buy-in, the mission fades. Setting the tone from the opening moment of
the year is an opportunity that should not be missed.

- Display the mission in highly visible ways throughout the district.

K-12 schools, especially public schools, do a remarkably poor job of branding themselves and can learn a great deal from their private school counterparts, universities, and the business sector.

Publicizing the school's mission statement as visibly as possible may seem superficial, but without it the school misses daily opportunities to boldly declare what it stands for and where it is headed.

- Start with the district and school websites, apps, and social media platforms. The mission, or at least the motto, should be a prominent feature near the top of each page.
- District letterhead, business cards, and presentations should all include the mission or motto.
- Conspicuously placed posters or murals in every classroom, office, and meeting space throughout the district should declare the school's mission and core beliefs for all to see.

3. Use the mission to drive personal and organizational decision-making.

As mentioned earlier, leaders of schools that are consistently recognized for high performance indicate a firm commitment to a collaboratively developed mission. That commitment leads to greater awareness and acceptance of the mission and core values by all members of the school community. School leaders should consider a variety of approaches to help their schools stay mission-focused:

- Encourage application of the mission and core values during decision-making processes.

Throughout the organization, decision-making must be centered on the mission, and each employee must understand their role in advancing that mission. Too often, schools operate as if only the professional educators (teachers and administrators) are responsible for carrying forward the academic and developmental mission of the district.

That is not true of high-performing schools, where everyone from bus drivers to payroll clerks understand how their work supports the district's goals. While teachers and administrators play the most visible role in driving the district toward its mission, every other employee in the district contributes in a meaningful way in that effort through effective, supportive completion of their daily tasks.

- Keep the mission at the forefront of decision-making processes.

Ensuring the mission is a focus at leadership team meetings, encouraging administrators and counselors to reference it when meeting with students, and asking all committees, task forces, student groups, and curriculum teams to identify how their work aligns to the school's mission are simple steps that reinforce the mission throughout the school.

Facilitating movement toward a mission-driven school is one of the foundational challenges for school leaders intent on creating a trust-filled organization. To attain that vision, leaders must begin at step one, the collaborative development of a mission statement, then take on the daily work of promoting that mission throughout all levels of the organization. Where there is a common understanding of "who we are and what we are about" there is greater trust in the intent of leaders throughout the organization.

Chapter 17

Planning for Trust

Almost any proposal a school leader puts forward will be met with support if adequate planning has fostered a sense of trust throughout the organization.

The importance of collaboratively identifying and consistently promoting a district-wide mission was identified in chapter 16 as a building block of a trust-filled school. Understanding and embracing the vision of what the school is and what it hopes to be provides staff, students, and community with common goals, consistent language, and core values that promote unity and trust throughout all sectors of the school community.

With a clearly stated mission identifying the destination, everyone is pulling in the same direction or, at the very least, clear on the direction in which the school is headed. By holding oneself accountable to the mission and encouraging others to hold themselves accountable to the mission, leaders allow all constituents to trust that the school is committed to its core values.

While the mission is the 20,000-foot view of the school's work, long-term strategic planning results in a ground-level perspective that is critical to the school's success. Effective planning provides the community with a roadmap that leads to the achievement of the mission, identifying challenges and opportunities, as well as preferred action steps for addressing the school's needs.

With input from all constituents, a thoughtfully constructed strategic plan becomes the reference point that drives decision-making during curriculum discussions, budget deliberations, and program review. When embarking on the development of a strategic plan, school leaders should aim to ensure the presence of several characteristics:

- Mission-focused: The plan must support the mission, and any action strategies identified must be directed at advancing the mission in meaningful ways.
- Concise: In order to be implemented, the plan must be easily digestible by those engaging in the work as well as those observing the progress.
- Implementable: While the plan's goals may be aspirational in nature, the strategies identified must be within the capacity of the organization, while encouraging growth and advancement.
- Measurable: Each action identified in the plan should be accompanied by quantifiable benchmarks and outputs that allow for easy identification and reporting to the community.
- Flexible: Even the best-developed plans cannot foresee events that may impact the organization even one year down the road. While multiyear planning is a necessity, the plan should allow for flexibility to address the unpredicted.
- Well-paced: A five-year plan should allow for work to be distributed over time, rather than expecting all actions to be completed in the first year or two. Recognizing the great effort required to make change, the plan should provide those doing the work with the time frame in which to do it well.

There are many ways to tackle the development of a long-term plan, including hiring facilitators, following templates provided through online sources, or crafting an in-house process that makes use of existing resources within the schools. Different approaches work to varying degrees of success depending on the climate and personalities present in the schools, but every planning process should possess several key traits that lead to a universally adopted product:

- Well-defined: A formally adopted charge from the school board, articulating the goals, responsibilities, composition, and authority of the planning committee is the first step in ensuring the process will be efficient and effective.
- Representative: Planning team composition that allows for participation from a range of constituents is critical to widespread understanding and buy-in of the plan.
- Interactive: Providing multiple touch points at various stages of the process with the staff and community ensures the plan is developed with a high level of engagement and input.
- Informed: Reviewing a vast yet manageable array of existing data provides the planning team with a knowledge base that promotes logical decision-making.

• Concentrated: A clear, concise timeline for the overall process, along with a well-defined agenda and time frame for all meetings, keeps the process moving and promotes ongoing participation.

DEFINING THE WORK

The charge from the school board is a critical first step in the planning process. The simple act of charging a committee to develop the strategic plan indicates the importance of this work and the board's commitment to it. The charge should include a definition of what is being created (e.g., "a five-year strategic plan for the school district to include, at a minimum, statements of mission and core beliefs, measurable goals, actions for meeting those goals, and reporting recommendations"), the composition of the planning team, engagement of the community, progress reporting, and the board's authority to edit, adopt, and distribute the plan.

REPRESENTATION

School leaders should carefully consider the composition of the team to ensure greater buy-in of the final plan. It may be easier to craft a plan without some representatives in the room, but a plan that is not well-received by the community won't be a plan that earns buy-in at the level needed to be successful. It is better to spend the time up front constructing a representative planning team and gathering input from a diverse group, than to construct a plan with limited input and, therefore, limited agreement.

It is critical for the planning team to understand its authority with regard to plan adoption and publication. As elected officials, the school board should retain the right to edit and distribute the plan as it sees fit. In a healthy district where trust has been fostered over time, the board is unlikely to make many edits to the work of the team, but it is vital that a clear statement of responsibility is made at the outset of any work, to avoid misunderstandings moving forward.

INPUT

Three opportunities for formal input from staff and community provide the planning team with more than enough information to determine if they are on the right track toward developing a plan that will be embraced, or, at a minimum, accepted by the vast majority of constituents. The first opportunity can be in the form of a survey seeking general input regarding the concerns and hopes of each respondent. The survey should be sent to all parents and students (as appropriate for their age), as well as to all staff and members of the community. This initial data will identify topics that are worthy of consideration.

Two rounds of input from the larger community may be provided through public and staff forums held at critical junctures in the planning process. One round of forums should be held early on in the process, once the team has an understanding of the data that will drive the planning process. Relevant data and a broad overview of the planning process and goals can be shared at each forum. Feedback at this point may help the team refine its approach to the process and clarify goals that had not been previously identified.

A second round of forums should be held later in the process, when a draft of a plan has been crafted. This provides staff and community members an opportunity to provide input at the editing stages and ensures that no "big ideas" have been missed.

INFORMATION

Reviewing existing data must occur early in the process in order for the planning team to identify the needs of the district. Some of the first data to be reviewed fit under the heading of "Who we are" and refer to demographic, enrollment, and student performance data readily available from the district office.

In rapidly growing schools or those with changing demographics, understanding data that predicts "Where we are going" will also be helpful. This data may be harder to come by, requiring enrollment studies and projections with the help of experts outside of the school staff.

Finally, data that describes "What we want to be" includes information related to specific programs that might be considered for implementation. Data from districts whose performance provides aspirational goals, or regional, state, or national data that provide a reasonable baseline to which the school should be compared are useful at this stage.

CONCENTRATION

Strategic planning can be an exciting process for a school district. With proper leadership, the planning team can move efficiently through its agendas, engage constituents at critical junctures and create a concise, meaningful plan that brings clarity to the actions required to meet the mission. It can also be laborious, tedious, and mind-numbing if the team allows for filibusters, extensive wordsmithing, and individual airing of grievances throughout the process. To avoid getting bogged down in minutiae, the team should set clearly defined parameters for all meetings, including those of any subgroups that are formed as part of the process.

Abiding by an agreed-upon meeting length provides attendees with confidence that their time is valued, and the meeting will be run efficiently. With a defined endpoint, participants are better able to focus on the task at hand throughout the meeting. Without setting those parameters, team members can lose focus and become frustrated that time is being wasted. Over the long run, they may lose interest and disengage from the process. With an agreed-upon limit to meeting lengths (ninety minutes is advised), team members arrive at each session ready to work and maintain their energy not only during the meeting, but throughout the entire planning process.

COMPONENTS OF THE PLAN

Reviewing strategic plans from schools throughout the country, one will find that the contents are as varied as the composition of the districts themselves. Some plans consist of more than 100 pages of data, position statements, and detailed approaches to learning, while others are much more concise, big-picture plans that identify a handful of strategies to be employed each year. Neither approach is necessarily better or worse than the other. However, each strategic plan should contain several core components that provide the reader with a clear understanding of where the district is, where it hopes to go, and how it will measure success:

- Current data that helps define where the school is at this point in time
- Projected data that may identify areas of strength or concern
- Major categories to be addressed in the plan, with statements of purpose for each
- Action items to be completed within each category
- A timeline for completing each action item
- Performance targets that allow for measurement of progress
- A reporting protocol that defines how progress will be shared

Each of these components lends itself to generating greater trust in the school. Providing existing data as well as projected data demonstrates transparency. Identifying performance targets and reporting procedures demonstrates accountability. Proposing action steps and timelines for completion demonstrates commitment to the mission.

If targets have been set appropriately, with an eye on continual improvement, it is not likely that every target will be met each year. School leaders should be clear that striving to meet each goal is what drives the school toward continual improvement. Setting the targets too high may lead to discouragement or dismissal by many, so it is important that some targets are well within reach within the time frame of the plan, while others may be more aspirational.

Flexibility in recognizing that five-year targets may need to be adjusted as local factors change is an important characteristic in a trust-filled school. Helping the school board and community understand the need for continual adjustment of targets and timelines is a skill all school leaders should seek to develop.

Once the plan is adopted, a structure should be in place to provide ongoing updates to the school board and community regarding completion of the action steps identified in the plan. With targets identified that measure the impact of each action item, the transparency and accountability of school leadership in reporting on those targets is one more significant way in which trust can be developed with the community.

OPERATIONALIZING THE PLAN

Separate from the strategic plan, the school leader should prepare a five-year plan for the operational aspects of the school that anticipates changes in enrollment, demographics, and student needs. This plan should be updated annually and shared with the school board to help meet the "no surprises" standard identified earlier. This operational plan considers the action items in the strategic plan as well as existing data to chart a course for adjusting staffing, facilities, infrastructure, and transportation to meet the needs of the district.

This plan should include spreadsheets and narratives that explain the district's needs to the reader. In a school district with changing enrollment, be it growing or declining, this plan might show projected changes in staffing levels over time. In a district with aging facilities or systems, the plan might identify potential capital costs for the coming years. In a district with a significant transportation fleet, the plan might identify an annual replacement schedule. In essence, the plan should provide a comprehensive view of the potential changes in staffing and infrastructure that are likely to be experienced in the coming years.

Table 17.1 provides an excerpt of a school staffing plan for a school that is experiencing moderate growth. The top portion of the table provides

Table 17.1   Staffing Plan Excerpt

High School Students	Current Year	Year 1	Delta	Year 2	Delta	Year 3	Delta
Grade 9	143	142	–1	138	–4	164	26
Grade 10	152	144	–8	145	1	143	–2
Grade 11	102	157	55	145	–12	145	0
Grade 12	145	106	–39	157	51	145	–12
TOTAL	**542**	**549**	**7**	**585**	**36**	**597**	**12**
Teachers (in full-time equivalents, FTE)							
English	6.5	6.5	0	7	0.5	8	1
Mathematics	6.5	6.5	0	7	0.5	8	1
Social Studies	6	6	0	6.5	0.5	6.5	0
Science	6.5	6.75	0.25	7	0.25	7	0
World Language	4.8	4.8	0	5	0.2	5	0
Health/P.E.	2.5	2.5	0	3	0.5	3	0
Technology	1	1	0	1	0	1	0
Music	1.5	1.75	0.25	2	0.25	2	0
Theater	0.8	0.8	0	0.8	0	0.8	0
Art	2	2	0	2	0	2	0
TOTAL	**38.1**	**38.6**	**0.5**	**41.3**	**2.7**	**43.3**	**2**

projected enrollment increases for three years, showing the change (delta) in each grade level in each year. The lower portion of the table provides a view of projected staffing levels in each learning area, provided the enrollment numbers change as projected.

In a growing district, a plan such as this is met with little emotion from staff members, as no one in the school should feel that their job is in peril. In a district with declining enrollment, the plan may be received with much greater angst. Identifying areas within the district where reductions in force (RIF) may be made, staff members at the lower end of each RIF list begin to seek more stable employment elsewhere, which can lead to declining staff morale. Still, leaders in schools with declining enrollment are better off preparing the staff for any such changes well ahead of the budget season.

Table 17.2 provides an excerpt from a five-year capital improvement plan, identifying various components of the school facility that will be in need of repair or replacement based on projected life spans, with estimated costs provided.

While a more detailed plan for facilities maintenance will be kept in the school's facilities division, this overview provides school leaders and the community with the information they need to prepare for upcoming expenditures.

In a district where facilities are in need of expansion or renovation, a more comprehensive planning process—similar to the strategic plan—is necessary. Unlike the strategic planning process, which might be conducted with

Table 17.2   Capital Improvement Plan Excerpt, Projecting Costs of Replacement or Repairs

	Year 1	Year 2	Year 3	Year 4	Year 5
Roof repairs			12,000	15,779	1,730
Energy upgrades		135,140			
Exterior light post					2,900
Technology lease	112,970				
Painting	5,000	7,465	5,470		5,430
Auditorium stage painting					1,900
Auditorium curtains					
Propane burnisher					3,395
Kitchen equipment lease	26,692	26,692	26,692	26,692	
Floor repair				1,129	8,511
Primary school pavement sealing			3,528		
Middle School boiler repairs			6,020	1,158	
High School press box sound system					5,040

in-house resources and facilitation, the facilities plan should be developed with guidance from a qualified architectural and engineering firm.

Because facilities projects require significant community investment, they require significant community trust. School leaders should not leave the development of these projects, nor the arguments for their necessity, to chance. Following a public review process similar to that laid out for the strategic plan will ensure community input is received and valued, and greater buy-in of the school's plan will result.

With experience, school leaders will learn that long-term strategic planning is one of the most significant steps they may take to create trust throughout the school and the community. Critics of school programming and spending have less to complain about if they see a plan is in place based on verifiable data that has been widely accepted and approved by the community.

Moving from year to year with no long-term plan leaves adversaries an opening to criticize the leadership for a lack of foresight. Putting a plan in place gives elected officials and the public confidence that the schools are well-managed, and resources are being wisely allocated to protect the public's investment.

Part VI

PERSONAL TRUST

Chapter 18

Building Personal Trust through Self-Care

To care best for others, leaders must first take care of themselves.

To this point, much of this text has been dedicated to the things leaders must do to take care of students, staff, and community members in their constituency. There is no question that effort requires tremendous focus, energy, and time—along with the attributes and skills described throughout the previous chapters of this book. School leadership is a demanding profession that asks much of those who accept the challenge and is not something for the faint of heart.

Too often, school leaders become consumed by the demands of the job, falling prey to the temptation to try to "finish up" a never-ending job before heading home each day. Even when they do leave the office, their mind races as they go over all that needs to be done tomorrow. The compulsion to be on the clock "24/7/365" is not a healthy approach for the leader, and it leads to a breakdown in effectiveness as personal well-being suffers. To encourage improvement in this area, the focus of this chapter will turn from how leaders take care of others to how they care for themselves, for doing so is a critical component of successful leadership.

Many school leaders, like CEOs, business owners, and nonprofit managers, suffer from an inability to separate themselves from their work. Each day, weighty decisions must be made that will have significant impact on students and staff. This can lead to sleepless nights, distracted commutes, and disengagement in personal relationships. Add to the mix the public nature of the job—the potential for press coverage that may not present the school or the leader in the most complimentary light—and it is easy to see why the tenure for school leaders continues to be quite short.

Leaders who understand the need for self-care will be better able to care for others. They will be healthier, have more energy, and avoid burn out more successfully than those who fail to achieve balance in their professional and personal lives. Days, weeks, and eventually years can be eaten up tending to the minutiae of the job if leaders are not attentive to their own personal needs. In order to be at their best, leaders must remember that if they are not well themselves, they will not be able to do their best for the organization—and that means students, staff, and the community will suffer.

Anyone who has flown in a commercial airliner can see how this logic is applied when flight attendants provide the passengers with safety instructions just prior to take-off: "In the event of a loss of cabin pressure, oxygen will be provided by facemasks that will drop from the overhead compartments. Please secure your own facemask first, so you may then help others." The logic is the same for school leaders; in order to best help others, they must be healthy themselves: emotionally, physically, mentally, and spiritually.

The following ideas are presented to help leaders arrive at work each day with the necessary energy, alertness, and passion to do the work effectively and efficiently:

A REMINDER ABOUT TRUSTING OTHERS

The importance of trusting in the staff was emphasized in chapter 5 as one characteristic of an effective leader, and it is worth repeating here, for it is a critical step in creating the capacity needed to lead a school effectively. In order for school leaders to do the work they need to do, they must empower and trust employees to complete tasks and take on leadership roles in a variety of settings; the load of school leadership is simply too much for one person to bear.

By trusting the staff, the leader demonstrates respect for their opinions, confidence in their abilities, and faith in their commitment to the school. By demonstrating trust, leaders reduce the likelihood that they will be micromanaging the staff, leaving themselves more time to perform their own tasks and creating space in their personal calendar for personal wellness activities. On an intangible note, trusting in others also allows for a decluttering of the mind, as the leader is no longer obsessing about minor details that are capably handled by others.

GET SOME SLEEP

It is well known that lack of sleep leads to a wide variety of health challenges. Obesity, heart disease, a weakened immune system, and mental health concerns are among the most common long-term impacts, while moodiness, memory loss, and low energy are some of the more immediate effects. Nobody wants to work for a leader displaying those qualities—and no leader should relish displaying them.

Every school leader will experience times when the recommended seven to nine hours of sleep is difficult to come by. A complex student discipline issue or a conflict with the school board can certainly trigger tossing and turning at night, just as a positive, energizing night watching students win an exciting game, perform courageously in the school musical, or present their learning at a school board meeting can provide an adrenaline rush that also makes sleep elusive. With so many opportunities for conflict or triumph in the school leader's typical week, and so many demands for late night and early morning meetings, finding the time to sleep can be challenging.

While there are many tips for improving sleep patterns for the general public, one of the most challenging for school leaders is to "turn off the screens." Unfortunately, school leaders are as glued to their cell phones as everyone else. After-hours checking of emails, texting with staff, posting announcements on social media or websites—all these activities keep leaders wed to their devices, consuming hours on evenings and weekends.

Blue light from laptops, cell phones, and other electronic devices stimulates the brain and interrupts sleep patterns. Turning off devices at least an hour prior to bedtime promotes relaxation. No constituent should expect a response to an email late at night, and school leaders should set the parameter that they are off the clock at a reasonable hour. Disengaging from business well ahead of bedtime, turning attention to a good book, a game of cards, a child's activity, or any sort of mindful relaxation will lead to better sleep patterns, greater energy during the day, and more effective leadership.

COMPARTMENTALIZE

School leaders are notoriously distracted spouses, partners, and parents. With so many responsibilities at work, there will always be a school-related situation to worry about. While focusing on complex problems is necessary, allowing them to get in the way of personal relationships brings about resentment and unhappiness at home, which leads to less effectiveness at work. Finding the balance between giving the job the attention it warrants and enjoying personal relationships that make life fulfilling is a challenge at which many school leaders fail—and they often fail in the wrong direction, putting school matters before family concerns.

Priding oneself on being a "workaholic" is a folly no school leader should embrace, and working smarter should be valued over working longer. Being able to leave work issues at work on a consistent basis is a skill leaders must develop if they are to be content at home and effective at school. Setting boundaries prevents resentment of the job and honors the need for personal and family time.

Unplugging at certain times of day, as suggested above to improve sleep patterns, also promotes better focus at home. While keeping up with email and messages may be necessary on the weekend, leaders should limit that work to a designated time. Early mornings before family members are active can be a good time to complete vital correspondences and stay apprised of unanticipated concerns, providing peace of mind on Saturdays and Sundays that allows the remainder of the day to be focused on family and personal interests.

On a daily basis, the commute home provides an opportunity to draw that line between work and personal life. Whether the commute is five minutes or an hour, the leader should identify a point at which thoughts turn away from work and focus on personal responsibilities and enjoyment. The work will be there when the time comes to return one's focus to school matters.

GET MOVING

Exercise may be the most significant activity missing from a school leader's life. Many claim there are just not enough hours in the day, and that may often be true. However, there are several strategies that should be considered to help school leaders get moving on a more consistent basis:

1. Hold mobile meetings.

Sitting still for lengthy periods of time is unnecessary for otherwise mobile individuals. Holding one-on-one or small group meetings while standing or walking, if possible, accomplishes two goals: (a) it promotes movement and good health, and (b) it leads to shorter meetings and more efficient use of time. Traveling through the school, so long as nothing confidential is being discussed, also promotes visibility for the school leader.

Superintendents who meet individually with principals on a regular basis should consider a mobile meeting to promote wellness and provide themselves with opportunities to engage with staff and students in informal ways. Principals can use this format to accomplish several tasks at once, that is, completing the necessary meeting and providing supervision throughout the building.

2. Travel the campus.

Many school leaders neglect to take advantage of opportunities to move throughout the day. Leaders with buildings in a campus setting should consider travelling routes that may be nearly as efficient as driving the car from one school to another. Principals should set aside times to move throughout the school—inside and out—during the academic day. One quick trip around the school will lead to greater productivity when leaders return to their desks, having stepped up their heart rate for a few minutes.

3. Find the time.

Aside from all of the benefits of exercise itself, early morning exercise leads to better sleep patterns at night. In order to feel better throughout the day and sleep more soundly at night, school leaders may want to consider getting out of bed thirty minutes earlier several mornings each week to get a quick workout in before going to school.

Another strategy is to work out at the school, or at a nearby facility, between the end of the school day and any evening meetings. Too often, school leaders remain at the office during that time, sedentarily sitting at their desk, hammering away at work before heading to a meeting. There's almost nothing healthy about sitting for long hours, possibly eating poorly, and staring at a screen, overly focused on work. School leaders must learn to separate from the job at various points during the day; finding the time to do something for personal wellness is critical to long-term health and productivity.

4. Adopt a mindset that it can be done.

There may not be enough hours in *every* day to engage in personal wellness to the extent one might like, but there are most likely enough hours in the *week* to do so. In other words, this does not need to be an everyday thing—not at the start, anyway. Finding one half-hour a couple of days each week and adding in some personal wellness on the weekends is a great way to start this effort. Too often, New Year's resolutions or spurts of inspiration lead to an "all-in" mentality that leads to injuries or burn-out, whereas a moderate approach to increasing participation in fitness activities will whet the appetite and help new participants stay motivated.

5. Consolidate through scheduling.

School leaders often fall into the trap of scheduling every meeting on separate days, chewing up evenings with lengthy meetings that should not take as much time as they do. Finding ways to consolidate the schedule provides sanity for the leader and is eventually appreciated by others as well.

One example of this at the superintendent's level would be to schedule subcommittee meetings of the school board on the same evening as the regular board meeting, but two hours earlier. For example, if the board meeting begins at 7:00 p.m., the monthly policy meeting could begin at 5:00. This way, two meetings are completed, but only one evening is spent at work—for both the superintendent and committee members—and the Policy Committee meeting is limited to a productive ninety minutes, providing a break for a snack or a walk between the two settings.

Meetings that drag on for hours produce diminishing returns. With a natural time constraint in place members come to the table ready to work, and the leader's effectiveness in moving the agenda toward successful completion is appreciated.

If possible, leaders should schedule meetings within the school day or earlier in the morning. While events such as public forums and school board meetings should take place in the evening to promote community participation, most other meetings can be scheduled at a time that is more convenient for the participants. Too often, school leaders fall into the habit of scheduling evening meetings, when a morning meeting may actually work better for everyone's schedule.

6. Make wellness an organizational goal.

Many organizations have come to understand the benefit of a healthy workforce. Schools are no different, and school leaders should communicate that understanding and model personal wellness for the staff. Setting up a wellness program indicates to the staff the importance with which school leaders view this work.

Healthier teachers are at work more consistently, giving students their best effort. Healthier employees in the school means fewer absences, lower substitute teacher costs, fewer transmissions of illnesses to students, and, in the long term, lower healthcare costs for employees and lower health insurance premiums for the school.

School leaders must set aside the belief that schools only promote development of the mind and recognize the need for students and staff to develop healthy practices for their bodies as well. Promoting and participating in wellness programs allows the leader to model for all constituents what good health looks like.

7. Engage with students.

School leaders have unique opportunities to engage in wellness activities as part of their regular workday. Throwing on a pair of sneakers and hopping into a physical education class, joining students in a game of four-square at recess, taking a walk around the school with students during their lunch break, working out in the fitness room after school—each setting provides its leader with specific opportunities to engage with students and accomplish personal wellness goals at the same time. Finding those opportunities to interact with students will make the day more enjoyable and the leader more productive.

BE INTENTIONAL ABOUT WHERE YOU LIVE

Setting boundaries and personal goals is critical for the health of the school leader. What works for one may not work for others. One school leader with young children may commit to living in the community in which they work to make participation in school and family activities at the same time possible, while another may find the separation of work and private activities is made easier by living in a different community.

These are personal decisions that should be made with a great deal of forethought. While engagement in the community is a priority for one, autonomy at home may be more important for another. Understanding one's own preferences prior to making such decisions is important for maintaining a healthy work-life balance.

DEVELOP HOBBIES UNRELATED TO WORK

Reading, traveling, exercise, playing music, writing, performing community service; school leaders are not unlike any member of society when they consider the many activities available to them. Too often, lack of time is used as an excuse for not taking advantage of those opportunities, but it may be more about lack of prioritizing, personal motivation, and efficiency.

Engaging in just one activity that provides a break from the never-ending barrage of school issues will provide momentary relief from the stress of the job. School leaders should foster one or more of their own passions and seek ways to engage in those activities several times each week. Stepping away from the work allows for better engagement when the job calls for complete attention, reducing the likelihood that resentment of the work will develop over the long haul.

DON'T LET THE SCHEDULE DICTATE YOUR DIET

Long days, late nights, and back-to-back meetings can often lead to unhealthy eating habits. It is not uncommon for school leaders to rush from one meeting to the next with a cookie in one hand and their laptop in the other, stopping at a fast-food joint on the way home late in the evening to grab a hamburger and fries. This is surely an unhealthy approach that will lead to myriad health concerns.

A better approach is to plan meals carefully at the beginning of each week, taking the time to create options that will prevent snacking on unhealthy foods. Keeping a well-insulated bottle handy will promote proper intake of water throughout the day. Leaders who plan healthy meals and stay hydrated will feel more energetic and focused to get through the longest days of the year.

TAKE A MOMENT EVERY NOW AND THEN JUST FOR YOURSELF

Mindfulness is not just a fad; it is a necessity for school leaders. There are a lot of suggestions for how to best practice mindfulness, but almost all of them come down to a few simple strategies—stepping away from the hustle and bustle for a moment, taking some deep breaths, and focusing on something other than the tasks and challenges at hand.

While this may be difficult during the busiest of days, sixty seconds of controlled breathing and mind-clearing meditation may be just what a leader needs to take on the next trial. Finding the right approach may be as simple as downloading a mindfulness app on a laptop or smartphone, or as complex as reading a helpful book or engaging with a consultant. Either way, the effort will be worth it if it leads to a healthier mindset.

Personal wellness is too often overlooked by school leaders, but poor health—be it physical, intellectual, emotional, or spiritual—results in the leader being less effective. Imbalance in personal and professional responsibilities can lead to a breakdown in trust at home, at work, and with oneself.

Being intentional about personal wellness requires discipline and planning, but the payoff is significant. Making the commitment to one's own health is not selfish; it benefits loved ones, colleagues, and students as well. Finding ways to focus on personal wellness even on the busiest of days will make stressful situations more manageable and lead to greater productivity.

Chapter 19

Being the Type of Leader You'd Like to Follow

School leadership is not rocket science but that doesn't mean it's easy.

None of the ideas and strategies shared in this book were developed as the result of superior intellect. They are merely a collection of approaches observed and developed over more than three decades in school-based leadership positions, assembled here as one practitioner's offering for others to consider. As noted in chapter 4, it is not knowing *what* to do that is difficult in most school leadership situations—it is having the personal resolve and interpersonal skills to pull it off. That resolve and those skills should be continually strengthened and honed throughout one's career so that they may develop into the school leader they originally aspired to be.

School leaders who come to be trusted in their school communities display many common personal and professional characteristics and employ a consistent set of practices in their schools, many of which have been discussed in previous chapters. A summary of those skills and strategies is shared here as a practical approach for school leaders' intent on becoming the type of leader others will want to follow.

PERSONAL BEHAVIOR IS THE STARTING POINT

Trust in the school begins with trust in the leader. To foster trust in themselves, leaders must first demonstrate trust in others by encouraging the sharing of ideas, creating a safe place for discussion and experimentation, and allowing staff members to exhibit personal competence and professionalism. Leaders who endeavor to lead without trusting will find themselves overwhelmed by the magnitude of the job, spending too much time at work, unable to delegate to others, and micromanaging staff. Those who trust their staff to get the job done will expand their own capacity to lead for innovation and organizational improvement.

EMPATHY AND INTEGRITY

Leaders who practice empathy and integrity in all situations provide constituents with confidence that they will be held to a consistent standard while being treated fairly, humanely, and with dignity. Remembering what it is like, or being able to understand what it is like, to walk in others' shoes, leaders are more likely to make decisions that are widely understood as being in the best interests of the school. Being a consistent voice for, and model of, what the school stands for provides constituents with confidence that the leader will do what is best in every situation.

RESTRAINT, COMPOSURE, AND COURAGE

Those who restrain from reacting too quickly in personal interactions offer a steady, calming influence in challenging situations, while those who restrain from starting a new initiative with each passing bandwagon give staff confidence that they are being led with thoughtful deliberation. New programs, methods, and approaches to learning are presented almost daily in the life of a school leader. While some may have great merit, many are presented by those who are looking to capitalize on others' implementation. Leaders must be careful about moving too quickly or letting their enthusiasm for a new idea blind them to the potential pitfalls.

Becoming personally invested in the adoption of one's own plan is a surefire way to diminish trust, as others soon understand that their perspective is not going to have an impact on the decision. Successful school innovation almost always comes from someplace other than the office, and the most adept school leaders ensure that their own ideas are co-opted and improved by others well before implementation occurs.

Courage is an underappreciated characteristic of school leaders. Almost nothing about the job of school leadership requires great intellectual powers, but nearly every situation requires personal and professional willpower. From holding honest discussions with teachers who must improve their instructional strategies to facing parent criticism of a student disciplinary matter, knowing what to do is not the challenge for most school leaders; it is the ability to do so with conviction and clarity.

STAFF TRUST IS FOSTERED THROUGH
INTENTIONAL PRACTICES

Giving staff the gift of time is one of the most appreciated trust-building actions school leaders can take. Reducing the frequency and length of staff meetings (and canceling meetings for which the agenda is of minimal importance) demonstrates understanding of the demands on their time. Leaders who avoid the need to "stand and deliver" and who provide teachers time to do their own important work will find staff members more willing to engage in discussions around new programming, rather than offering up resistance due to an already-full plate of responsibility.

MANAGEMENT AS A CORE
COMPETENCY OF LEADERSHIP

Ensuring the school is well-led requires ensuring the school is well-managed. Teachers value structure and consistency, which provide safety and security on many levels. While management is the low-hanging fruit of leadership, it is important to take good care of those tasks that provide staff with the sense that a steady hand is guiding the school.

SHARED LEADERSHIP

Teacher voice is one of the most critical features of a high-trust school. While almost every school has structures in place that give the appearance of collaborative leadership, authentic shared leadership is found only in those schools where trust has been continually fostered through all manner of interpersonal and organizational communications. From program reviews to professional development, teachers should be invited not only to participate but to lead improvement efforts, as they are on the front lines working with students every day and are best positioned to understand the needs and the likely outcomes of each effort.

STUDENT TRUST

Effective school leaders put student needs first without concern for their own resume, building trust through collaborative efforts that focus on school-wide improvement. While the community appreciates a leader who fixes the "broken windows" quickly and efficiently, larger school improvement efforts require the trust that the leader is taking care of students, first, while being considerate of staff needs and community perspectives at the same time.

Students learn and work better when trust is at the core of the school. From the moment they are welcomed to the school each day, kept safe by consistent and empathetic application of fair standards, and empowered by equitable access to high-quality programming, students yearn for trust in every setting. Leaders have their greatest impact on student learning by creating a culture of trust that permeates every layer of the school.

EQUITY TAKES EFFORT

A deliberate approach to equity is required of school leaders if they are to maximize student learning. This goes well beyond providing the same opportunities for all students, requiring a thorough review of policies, practices, and curriculum to ensure individual and institutional bias are acknowledged and eradicated. This will be school-wide work that requires a tremendous level of trust among all who participate, as it may be challenging for some to come to terms with their own unintended biases.

A LEADER'S GREATEST IMPACT:
HIRING GREAT TEACHERS

Hiring highly effective, student-centered staff is the single most important job of the school leader. Imagine a school in which every single employee, including teachers, office staff, custodians, nutrition workers, and others, have adopted the school's mission and engage with every student in a caring, instructive manner. This is what school leaders should strive for as learning is maximized in a school full of employees who authentically like students and care deeply about their growth.

While it is unlikely a leader may have the opportunity to hire 100 percent of the employees at the school, they will be responsible for supervising and nurturing staff to be the type of educator students need. Engaging onboarding of new hires and effective supervision of veteran staff is critical for the improvement of instruction and an area in which school leaders should invest significant time. Ensuring that high standards are not being confused with rigidity is a fine line school leaders walk each day and trusting relationships with teachers lead to trusting relationships with students.

COMMUNITY TRUST IS CRITICAL

School leaders must be deliberate about fostering trust with families by communicating clearly and effectively in all situations. While over-communicating can lead to dismissal of school notices, under-communicating will almost always lead to a decimation of trust in the school. A strong communications plan, with agreed-upon protocols for who is responsible for each type of notice, is necessary to provide the community with the information it needs.

Handling criticism can be a challenging dilemma for school leaders. It is important to remember that while educators may truly care for their students, their concern will not match the level of emotion that grows from a parent's love for their child. Being reflective about criticism can assist school leaders in their own growth, promoting preparedness and thoughtfulness that may not develop in a situation where critiques are not provided. It does not make criticism any more enjoyable to receive, but having some perspective as to why the complaints are being levied will help school leaders move toward personal growth as a result.

Working with the media, rather than taking a defensive posture, will foster trusting relationships that may be helpful when the inevitable difficult stories arise. School leaders who proactively share information or respond to media requests with helpful quotes will build capital that may be helpful when the school's story needs to be told.

TRUST AMONG LEADERS SETS THE TONE

Whether working at the district level or within the school, leaders are charged with working with others (school boards or leadership teams) to set the direction for the school. Effective teams are clear on their roles and responsibilities, understanding when collaboration with others is necessary while communicating consistently with the school community. Setting a tone of professionalism and cooperation, ensuring efficient use of time and resources, and collecting and distributing information is the responsibility of the leader.

MISSION MATTERS

Schools with a concise, collaboratively developed mission statement, along with widely distributed and commonly understood core values, create a firm foundation on which to base decision-making throughout the school. It is the responsibility of the school leader to ensure that the mission statement is not theirs alone but one that is adopted with much input from all constituents and drives programming, policies, and practices in all areas of school life.

Organizational planning must be an ongoing consideration of a mission-focused school. Without proper planning, the school may or may not progress toward its goals, falling prey to distractions and inconsistencies. With collaboratively developed and broadly communicated goals and core values, schools maintain a course of continual improvement, which is important for even the highest performing organizations.

PERSONAL CARE IS A MUST

There is no substitute for good health. School leaders must be deliberate about caring for themselves physically, emotionally, mentally, and spiritually. Identifying strategies and times for self-care are critical to the long-term success of each leader. Part of self-care goes all the way back to personal behaviors and one's ability to trust in others. Leaders who trust others provide themselves with more time to care for themselves, which allows them to care better for others.

The people-oriented business of schools requires that trust be built through interpersonal interactions and communications with all members of the school community. Every interaction a school leader has with constituents, be it with staff members, students, parents, community members, or media personnel, is an opportunity to increase trust in the organization. When mishandled, those interactions may also result in diminished trust. It is up to the school leader to ensure that trust is fostered through thoughtful, deliberate actions such as those described throughout this book.

A wise mentor once said to his charges, "No two days will ever be the same. Every day, you will either be better or worse than you were the day before; push yourself to be better than you were yesterday." That is the challenge facing school leaders. The demands of the job ensure that no two days are exactly the same; leaders must plan, respond, and communicate with versatility and adaptability as they focus on continual improvement.

Understanding that interpersonal trust is the critical component of organizational performance, school leaders have the opportunity (and responsibility) to face each day with a commitment to personal growth that will lead to a deeper sense of trust through all levels of the organization. Leaders who foster trust through intentional actions each day will create a climate shift in the school that results in greater innovation and creativity, higher levels of engagement from staff and students, and stronger community support.

Of course, not every situation a school leader may encounter has been covered in this text. Indeed, the vast array of interactions a school leader has even in a single day cannot be covered in a text of this length. What has been shared here, though, provides a solid foundation on which to build the skills and characteristics necessary to set a course for successful school leadership. The challenge is not in understanding but in implementation.

Effective school leadership requires continual focus and effort. Leaders must start by trusting in others and dedicating themselves to practices that demonstrate empathy and integrity in every interaction. Consistency of practice will result in greater trust in the leader, which will permeate all layers of the school. The final outcomes will include clearer understandings of the school's mission, healthier relationships among all constituents, and improved student learning.

Bibliography

Collins, J. C. *Good to Great: Why Some Companies make the Leap ... and Others Don't*. New York: HarperBusiness, 2001.

Covey, Stephen M. R. *The Speed of Trust*. New York: Free Press, 2006.

Covey, Stephen R. *The Seven Habits of Highly Effective People*. New York: Free Press, 1989. https://nces.ed.gov/programs/coe/indicator_clr.asp

Learning Policy Institute. Teachers of Color: In High Demand and Short Supply [Press Release]. April 19, 2018. https://learningpolicyinstitute.org/press-release/teachers-color-high-demand-and-short-supply

McDaniel, Terry & Gruenert, Steve. "The Making of a WEAK Principal." *School Administrator*. June 2018. http://my.aasa.org/AASA/Resources/SAMag/2018/Jun18/McDaniel_Gruenert.aspx#:~:text=On%20a%20typical%20day%2C%20a%20principal%20will%20make%20about%20300%20decisions

Public Trust in Government, 1958-2019. Pew Research Center, 2019. Washington, D.C. https://www.people-press.org/2019/04/11/public-trust-in-government-1958-2019/

Ryan, Liz. "Ten Ways To Build Trust On Your Team." *Forbes*, March 17, 2018. https://www.forbes.com/sites/lizryan/2018/03/17/ten-ways-to-build-trust-on-your-team/?sh=2faa762c2445

Reeves, Douglas. *From Leading to Succeeding*. Bloomington, IN: Solution Tree, 2016.

Trust and Distrust in America. Pew Research Center, 2019. Washington, D.C. https://www.people-press.org/2019/07/22/trust-and-distrust-in-america/

Zak, Paul. "The Neuroscience of Trust." *Harvard Business Review*. January–February, 2017. Harvard Business Publishing; all rights reserved. https://hbr.org/2017/01/the-neuroscience-of-trust

About the Author

Andrew Dolloff, PhD, is a thirty-five-year veteran of public schools, starting his career as a high school chemistry teacher before making the transition to school leadership in 1995. He has served as a high school principal and superintendent of schools throughout the Portland, Maine, region. In 2021, Andrew was named Maine's Superintendent of the Year, which followed his recognition in 2020 as the New England League of Middle Schools' Outstanding Superintendent. He was awarded the Outstanding Leadership Award by the Cumberland County Superintendents' Association in 2017 and was named Maine's High School Principal of the Year in 2004. Andrew has led two school districts that have been recognized for high performance and greater efficiency, with three different schools that have earned National Blue Ribbon recognition.

Andrew has served on the International Advisory Board for the Harvard Graduate School of Education's Principals' Center and as a board member at the New England School Development Council. He also sits on the advisory board for the University of Southern Maine's Educational Leadership program, where he is a lecturer of Educational Leadership, School Finance, and Contemporary Issues in Education.

Andrew's wife, Brenda, is also an educator of more than thirty-five years. They have four grown children, each of whom were educated in Maine's public schools before completing successful undergraduate and graduate programs throughout New England and heading off to their careers in finance, law, and business from Maine to California.

Andrew can be reached through LinkedIn at linkedin.com/in/andrew-do lloff-ph-d-maine.

Made in United States
North Haven, CT
03 July 2024

54368807R00104